顾问

姚伟彬　蓝志雄　刘润东　梁美儿

莫启明　彭执中　汤柏燊　黄承发

杨　柳　叶铭泉　张本梓　张美芳

摄影

许恒嘉；住宿式书院办公室、传讯部及Chiii Design提供

原排版及装帧设计　Chiii Design

Advisors

Iu Vai Pan, Lam Chee Shiong Desmond, Lau Yun Tung, Leung May Yee Janny,
Mok Kai Meng, Pang Chap Chong Paul, Kevin Thompson, Wong Seng Fat Alfred,
Yang Liu, Yeh Ming Chuan, Zhang Benzi, Zhang Meifang

Photography　Hsu Heng-chia; Residential College Offices, Communications Office,
　　　　　　　　and Chiii Design

Original page-setting and cover design　Chiii Design

住宿式书院
实践全人教育理念

澳门大学的探索

宋永华　苏基朗　黄兆琳　等编

ZHEJIANG UNIVERSITY PRESS
浙江大学出版社
·杭州·

图书在版编目（CIP）数据

住宿式书院实践全人教育理念：澳门大学的探索 /
宋永华等编. -- 杭州：浙江大学出版社，2022.9
ISBN 978-7-308-22830-5

Ⅰ.①住… Ⅱ.①宋… Ⅲ.①高等教育－教育研究－
澳门 Ⅳ.①G649.286.59

中国版本图书馆CIP数据核字（2022）第124414号

住宿式书院实践全人教育理念：澳门大学的探索

宋永华　苏基朗　黄兆琳　等编

策划编辑	吴伟伟
责任编辑	宁　檬
责任校对	陈逸行
封面设计	周　灵
出版发行	浙江大学出版社
	（杭州天目山路148号　邮政编码：310007）
	（网址：http://www.zjupress.com）
排　　版	浙江时代出版服务有限公司
印　　刷	浙江省邮电印刷股份有限公司
开　　本	889mm×1194mm　1/16
插　　页	2
印　　张	8
字　　数	240千
版 印 次	2022年9月第1版　2022年9月第1次印刷
书　　号	ISBN 978-7-308-22830-5
定　　价	150.00元

序 / Preface

　　澳门大学（以下简称澳大）作为澳门唯一的综合性公立大学，长期以来受到中央及特区政府和社会各界的关心和支持。自 1981 年创校以来，一直秉承"仁、义、礼、知、信"的校训，并通过其独特的教学模式和住宿式书院（以下简称书院）系统，形成以专业、通识、研习及社群教育为主的全人教育模式，建立了学院与书院相辅相成的协同育人教育体系，其中承担社群教育的书院系统更是本科生教育的最大特色。

　　澳大书院是一个知识整合的学习平台，体现了澳大四位一体的全人教育理念，力求培养学有所成以及情操高尚的大学毕业生。具体而言，书院系统旨在把学生培育成具有家国情怀的良好公民，具有社会责任感，遵纪守法、廉洁诚信，为澳门、中国乃至整个人类社会做出贡献。书院的社群生活及活动，旨在提升住宿生的七大胜任力，包括公民责任心、全球竞争力、知识整合能力、团队协作、服务与领导、文化参与及健康生活等。

　　住宿式书院，营造了充满启发性的环境，让学生得以互相学习，增广见闻，丰富生活；并且能培养学生的全球视野、独立思维能力及文化自信，学习如何与不同专业和文化的人共存、沟通、合作，借以了解毕业后真实的社会环境，准备好在全球化世界启航，提升自身的全球竞争力。书院有驻院及非驻院学术导师，除提供个人指导以外，亦开设可自由参加的导修课，内容包括专业知识、通识知识以及专业语文等，借以帮助学生融会贯通学术知识、慎思明辨、创新创业。

　　澳大在人才培养、科学研究、社会服务、对外合作等多方面不断进步，在中国及国际的声誉不断提升。澳大将继续积极配合特区政府的施政理念，进一步发展与优化其书院教育，发挥其在爱国爱澳人才培养方面的积极作用。未来，澳大将不断优化书院系统，继续构建全人教育环境，实践全人教育理念。

宋永华

校长

As the only public comprehensive university in Macao, University of Macau （UM） has received long-term support from the central government, the Macao Special Administrative Region （SAR） government, and all sectors of society. Since its founding in 1981, UM has adhered to the virtues of "Humanity, Integrity, Propriety, Wisdom, and Sincerity". It emphasises the holistic development of students by implementing a unique education model based on discipline-specific education, general education, research and internship education, and community and peer education, as well as an integrated education system in which faculties and residential colleges （RC） achieve synergy by complementing each other. In particular, the RC system is considered the jewel in the crown of UM's undergraduate education.

UM's RC system provides a platform for knowledge integration of the "4-in-1" education model with the aim of cultivating well-rounded graduates equipped with intellectual and moral capabilities. It nurtures students to become contributing members of the society committed to upholding the values of patriotism, social responsibility, law-abidance, integrity and honesty, and devoting themselves to Macao, China and humanity at large. The RC system strives to enhance students' seven competencies through communal living and activities, including responsible citizenship, global competitiveness, knowledge integration, teamwork collaboration, service and leadership, cultural engagement, and healthy lifestyle.

UM's RC creates a stimulating environment in which students can coexist, communicate and collaborate with people of different disciplines and cultural background, while maturing into culturally confident life-long learners who can think independently and creatively with global aware. The enlightening RC experiences further enable students to confront real-life challenges after graduation and prepare them better for a fruitful and sustainable career amid global competition. In addition, RC's resident and non-resident fellows are dedicated to conducting non-credit-bearing academic programmes composing of disciplinary studies, general education, and academic language skills, targeting to support students to better integrate academic knowledge, to think critically, and to excel and venture beyond limitations.

UM has made remarkable progress in nurturing professionals, scientific research, community service and international cooperation, with its rise in reputation locally, regionally and internationally. In line with SAR government's policy, UM actively engages in cultivating patriotic and affectionate talents through further enhancement of its RC education. In the future, UM shall continue its unceasing efforts to optimise the RC system, provide an environment conducive to academic excellence and pursue a whole-person education.

Yonghua Song
Rector

前 言 / Introduction

　　本书旨在说明澳大书院系统的起源、演进、愿景。澳大书院参考了哈佛、耶鲁等美国大学及牛津、剑桥等英国大学的不同类书院创办模式，同时继承了中国宋明书院的精神。澳大一直秉承"仁、义、礼、知、信"的校训，推行融合专业、通识、研习及社群教育等"四位一体"的教育模式，通过该独特的教育模式以及作为社群教育重点的书院系统，达到为学生提供全人教育的目的。澳大的教育使命是培养澳门、中国乃至世界发展所需之具有家国情怀、国际视野、全球竞争力和社会责任感的公民以及创新型人才。澳大书院系统在落实澳大全人教育理念上，扮演着极为关键的角色。

This book aims to document the origin, evolution and vision of the RC system at UM. The system is modelled on the house or RC system of Harvard and Yale in the US as well as the college system of Oxford and Cambridge in the UK, and has inherited the spirit of *shuyuan* (academy) during the Song and Ming dynasties in China. Adhering to the motto "Humanity, Integrity, Propriety, Wisdom, and Sincerity", the university's undergraduate education is structured on a 4-in-1 model integrating disciplinary education, general education, research and internship education, and community and peer education. This unique education model and the RC system, which is the core of the community and peer education, aim to foster the whole-person development of students. UM's education mission is to cultivate responsible citizens and innovative leaders who are strong in national commitment and global competitiveness, with international outlook, meeting the needs of the advancement of Macao, China, and the world. The RC system thus plays a critical role in realising the university's vision for whole person education.

目 录 / Contents

第一部分　中西住宿式书院教育的前世今生　　3
　第一章　中西书院教育的传统　4
　第二章　现代中西住宿式书院的发展　14

第二部分　试行及实践时期的澳大住宿式书院　　27
　第三章　缘起和理念　28
　第四章　组织及教育活动　38
　第五章　图说住宿式书院设施　54
　第六章　图说住宿式书院试行及实践时期的五大能力指标教育　65

第三部分　发展与优化时期的澳大住宿式书院　　79
　第七章　理念及设施　80
　第八章　教育机制及组织　88
　第九章　住宿式书院发展与优化时期七大胜任力教育　96
　第十章　教育绩效评估机制　106

结　语　110

参考文献　115

附　录　117

PART 1　College Education in China and the West in Historical Perspective　3

Chapter 1　The Traditions in Education　4

Chapter 2　Development of Modern Chinese and Western Residential Colleges　14

PART 2　Trial Run and Implementation Phase of UM Residential College Education　27

Chapter 3　Origin and Philosophy　28

Chapter 4　Organisation and Educational Activities　38

Chapter 5　Snapshots of Facilities in Residential Colleges　54

Chapter 6　Pictures Illustrating the Training of the Five Competencies during the Trial Run and Implementation Phase　65

PART 3　Development and Enhancement Phase of UM Residential College Education　79

Chapter 7　Concept and Facilities　80

Chapter 8　Education Programmes and Organisation　88

Chapter 9　Seven Competencies of RC Education during the Development and Enhancement Phase　96

Chapter 10　Education Performance Assessment　106

Concluding Remarks　110

Reference　115

Appendix　117

曹光彪书院
COLÉGIO CHAO KUANG PIU
CHAO KUANG PIU COLLEGE

郑裕彤书院
COLÉGIO CHENG YU TUNG
CHENG YU TUNG COLLEGE

张昆仑书院
COLÉGIO CHEONG KUN LUN
CHEONG KUN LUN COLLEGE

蔡继有书院
COLÉGIO CHOI KAI YAU
CHOI KAI YAU COLLEGE

霍英东珍禧书院
COLÉGIO DO JUBILEU DE PÉROLA HENRY FOK
HENRY FOK PEARL JUBILEE COLLEGE

吕志和书院
COLÉGIO LUI CHE WOO
LUI CHE WOO COLLEGE

马万祺罗柏心书院
COLÉGIO MA MAN KEI E LO PAK SAM
MA MAN KEI AND LO PAK SAM COLLEGE

满珍纪念书院
COLÉGIO MEMORIAL MOON CHUN
MOON CHUN MEMORIAL COLLEGE

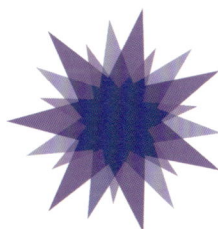

绍邦书院
COLÉGIO SHIU PONG
SHIU PONG COLLEGE

何鸿燊东亚书院
COLÉGIO DA ASIA ORIENTAL STANLEY HO
STANLEY HO EAST ASIA COLLEGE

第一部分 | PART 1

中西住宿式书院教育
的前世今生

College Education
in China and the West
in Historical Perspective

第一章

中西书院教育的传统

官私成立专门机构从事教育工作，古已有之，中西皆然。

先秦已有校、序、庠、辟雍、泮宫、大学、小学、塾等官学；秦汉至明清，复有中央的博士官、太学、国子监、弘文馆，地方的郡州县学等，不一而足。隋唐始行科举，宋至清渐成朝廷吸纳官员的主要途径，并辅以各级官办举业应试教育机构，诵习四书五经或程朱之教。

春秋战国孔门以四科六艺养君子，弟子三千；墨翟兼爱非攻以造贤士，门徒百计，皆私家教育的滥觞。六朝士族以家为塾，佛教寺院广立精舍，都是风行一时的私学。中唐以后始有书院之名，原意藏书籍的屋宇，类似佛教寺院的藏经阁，后变成诵习书籍的教育机构。宋初以科举取士，民间追求教育的应试者众多，私学如应天府书院等渐吸引大量学生，其中不少通过科举入仕。书院作为新兴私学组织，经宋代儒家巨擘的大力推崇，遂遍及各重要城市，部分则偏处乡郊或坐落于名山之麓，成为中国传统教育史上，官学以外培养文人及士大夫最重要的民间教育机构。

中国传统教育虽可分官学私学两种，但实际上两者有千丝万缕的关系。书院创办者、兴修者、讲学者、学生及其家人，往往是现任官员或具官员背景；著名书院往往获朝廷赐书、颁匾等认可；书院资产如学田等，除民间捐赠外，常由地方官府调拨。职是之故，私学难与官家脱钩。书院和科举的关系，亦无固定模式。开始时犹如官学般，为学生提供应试教育。后来科举内容渐渐公式化与政治化，部分书院的教育内容开始与科举或朝政分道扬镳。明末短期发展出以议政为主的书院；清代书院则多以举业为主，往往与官学无异。一方面，书院教育重在名师讲学，答问释疑，生员则诵习精读，切磋论辩，修身笃行。强调为学目的不谋功名而求济世的书院，不必囿于举业课程，故此，讲学者可以从心讲学，追求至善，生员来去自由，悉从其便，书院的教育环境因而相当灵活。但另一方面，书院以名师凝聚生徒，讲究师承门派，学生有时亦不免流于墨守师说，同类相聚，排拒异己新见。

总而言之，中国传统教育不论官私，都兼重品格与学问。学业的内容，又多以儒家经典及三纲五常伦理知识为主，兼通文史，并且涉猎子学，包含哲学、数理、农务、货殖、技艺、营造等所谓百家之学。因此，优秀传统知识分子多通才博识，为官则通经致用，经世济民；乡居则习律行医，修梁筑堰，教化兴学，和合乡里。在这个教育传统中，最具代表性的宋明书院，除经史子集等授受之外，尤重修身德行。例如作为书院教育宗师的南宋理学泰斗朱熹，主张格物致知，诚意正心，然后可言修齐治平。个人修养与对万物知识的追求，相辅相成。对家庭社会的贡献，正是为学的出发点。概括而言，中国传统教育，一向道德学问并举，通博专精互济。宋明书院则尤其重视培养学生的心性品格，作为求学的基础。

宋代名书院中，影响最广的是白鹿洞书院，延续至今仍具高等学府功能的如岳麓书院。前者在今天江西九江市庐山之下；后者在湖南长沙市岳麓山之下。白鹿洞书院藏有南宋理学名家朱熹 1179 年出任知南康军（今庐山市）时所制定的《白鹿洞书院揭示》，或名《白鹿洞书院学规》。这套被奉为历代书院教育规章典范的学规，开宗明义，即说书院教育，旨在教授学生父子、君臣、夫妇、长幼、朋友间的五种伦理知识，即所谓五教。学生学习的五序为博学、审问、慎思、明辨、笃行。学、问、思、辨用于彻底了解相关的知识道理。笃行即知识与行为要贯通一致。具体来说笃行亦有修身、处事、接物三个要旨。修身的要旨在言忠信，行笃敬，惩忿窒欲，迁善改过。处事的要旨是正其义不谋其利，明其道不计其功。接物的要旨为己所不欲，勿施于人；行有不得，反求诸己。这套典范性的学规，说明书院教育应以道德伦常之道为教育终极目标，让学生通过学问思辨等学习手段，追求对相关道德知识的心领神会。同时，道德知识不能停留在认知阶段，必须付诸实践。在实践时学生亦有修身（自身修养）、处事（解决问题）及接物（与人相处）三方面的若干大原则，可资遵从。

　　岳麓书院，976 年潭州（今长沙）太守朱洞在佛教寺学原址上所建，宋真宗召见山长周式赐院名御额，得以名扬天下。南宋时因理学大儒张栻执教以及他与朱熹1167 年会讲辩论《中庸》，声名复振，时人誉为四大书院之一。朱熹 1194 年奉职潭州时，兴复和扩充了岳麓书院，亲自讲学，可能同时引入了他的学规，有谓生员曾达千人。书院历元明清三代虽迭有兴废，但不断得到官私修复，不致湮没。在帝制时期，岳麓书院的教育传统，始终以培养道德高尚而又能经世济民的士大夫为宗旨，并且培育了一代又一代的湘湖才俊如曾国藩等，学问事功，名传于世。晚清改学制时，废书院为学堂，废科举，行西式新学制。岳麓书院又经历了湖南高等学堂（1903 年）、湖南大学（1926 年）、国立湖南大学（1937 年）、湖南大学（1959 年）等校制、学制变迁。1986 年湖南大学的岳麓书院重修工程告竣，成为湖南大学成员单位之一，以"岳麓书院"为名，其内陆续设立文化研究所及历史、哲学、考古等本、硕、博专业课程。根据简介，湖南大学强调在长期办学历程中继承和发扬"传道济民、爱国务实、经世致用、兼容并蓄"的教育传统，并以"基础扎实、视野开阔、德才兼备"为人才培养的总目标。

西方教育制度滥觞于古希腊城邦的派地亚教育（paideia）。paideia 涵义甚广，包括文化、文明、文教、教化等意思。与中国由官学发展成官私并行的轨迹迥然有别，希腊城邦中受贵族政权支持的军事教育，演变成非军事的民间教育，并以雅典教育为典范。前期多由个别老师（didaskalos）招收贵族为主的学生传授体育、书写和艺术等技艺与知识，借以培养德智兼备的"君子素质"（kalos kagathos）。5 世纪以后，派地亚系统渐出现类似学校规模的学园（scholé），教育内容扩充到文法、逻辑、修辞、哲学、伦理学、演讲、雄辩、音乐、艺术、算术、几何、天文、地理、历史、政治及体育等知识领域。其中文法、逻辑、修辞渐形成三艺（trivium），为身份相对于奴隶的自由民（liberalis）所应具的知识；再进一步便应学习天文、算术、几何、音乐，即四艺（quadrivium）。两者构成以七艺（ars）为主体的博雅教育（ars liberalis），旨在培育通博而有能力探索宇宙和人生真理的德智双全的自由民，亦称 enkuklios paideia。Enkuklios 有周全、循环、普通、寻常等意思，即全面人格的教育，或全人教育。其中部分学园，渐成著名教育机构，兼具研究学问、论辩真理、收藏图书文献等功能，如柏拉图设立的 Academy（柏拉图学园）、亚里士多德成立的 Lyceum（亚里士多德学园）等。罗马希腊化教育遍及帝国各地，往往由官方出资，继承希腊派地亚系统，崇尚人文素养（humanitas），一般包括所谓七艺的博雅教育，同时融合了罗马社会自公元前 5 世纪颁布《十二铜表法》以来一贯强调的法律传统。罗马的人文教育，同样旨在培育德智双全的自由罗马公民。

5 世纪西罗马帝国覆亡，欧洲中古时代揭幕，前期重要的教育机制转移至基督教修道院，通过古文献的抄写训练，培育精通希腊罗马经典著作以及圣经释义的修士僧侣，其品德要求仍不离高尚贞洁、慈爱行善的基督教伦理。经过几百年混战，上至希望号令天下的神圣罗马帝国及罗马教廷，下至各地城邦、诸侯、王国，均逐渐形成各自在政治和社会方面的权威体制。在此政权林立的格局之下，各地因其所需，涌现了各种各样的教育机构，或地方政权运营的学校、教会学校、专业行会学校，或学生教师共同经营的私塾等。12 世纪之后，演化出一类

高等教育体制，称为大学（universitas），此为西方教育史上划时代的大事，奠定了西方高等教育的基本格局，至今影响无远弗届，成为全球通行的高等教育体制。

大学的特色是在特定社区内，一群包括教师或学生的法定社团，通过政权或教皇的诰命、敕许等方式获得认可和授权，根据自身的章程和宪章，自治管理学校事务，传授法定的学问知识，并在学生通过法定的考试后，授予学士、硕士或博士学位。大学的地理位置较固定，往往以所在地的名称为名。学生和教师则往往来自欧洲各地，但享有当地法定的各种生活特权。教育内容几乎无关本地掌故，集中教授希腊罗马教育以来具有普世或普遍意义的人文学、神学、法学及医学。学位资格通用于欧洲各地，毕业生可在各地学校执教。因此早期成功的大学，都是开放式及普世型的。最著名的是博洛尼亚大学、巴黎大学及牛津大学。博洛尼亚大学被认为是欧洲最早的大学，据说成立于 1188 年，年份虽有争议，但 13 世纪初博洛尼亚大学无疑已经具备所谓大学的特点，且以法学院及法学为主。13 世纪初，巴黎大学及牛津大学亦是在 11 世纪、12 世纪地方教会学校等的基础上，逐渐演化成大学，由教授基础学问的人文学院（facultatis artium），以及作为进修学院的神学院、法学院及医学院三所高级学院（superior faculties）组成，其中以神学院享誉最隆。另外，13 世纪初牛津大学的一批教师移居剑桥市另建了一所学校，以"剑桥"命名，与牛津大学结构类似，并成为与牛津大学不相伯仲的大学。剑桥大学四学院中，神学院及哲学专业最佳。

与巴黎大学一样，13 世纪牛津大学、剑桥大学渐成体系，因为学生和教师多非本地人，他们向当地居民租赁住所则时生抵牾，甚至弄出人命，因此，需要为师生安排住宿，由此产生了一种教育机构，其可以自我管理和拥有一定财产，初称 hall，或 house，后多称为 college。Hall 古英语中表示客舍，拉丁语为 hospitium；House，拉丁语为 domum，原意亦泛指居家。两词当时演变成提供师生住宿的一种法定教育宿舍。College 拉丁语为 collegium，原意为有法定地位的团体（corporation）。

至此三个词都表示为师生提供住宿的一种法定教育机构。对于牛津大学及后来剑桥大学的college、house 及 hall 来说，如果译作"学院"的话，则与同样译作"学院"的 faculty 重复。西方教育史著作中一般译作"学舍"。中国学界讨论牛津大学和剑桥大学的学院制时，常常称为"书院"，以别于"学院"。故本书沿用较通行的译名，称作书院。这些大学成员书院，由于可为教师提供住所及拥有各种法定特权，吸引了各地学有所长和享有盛誉的学者加盟。教学功能不亚于大学直属的学院及其学系，内容亦不离学院所授的人文学、法学、医学及神学。不过由于师生在书院同宿共膳，作息相同，教师可以对学生耳提面命，言传身教，有学院讲学达不到的教育效果。当然书院教师往往同时受聘于学院，学生除受业于所属书院教师外，同时受业于学院受聘的其他书院名师。学院和书院，从专业教育角度而言，各司其职，但相辅相成，相得益彰。而作为一所大学关键功能的考试和颁授学位权限，仍由大学和学院掌握。书院有教育之实，而无颁授学位之权。

以牛津大学三间最古老书院之一的墨顿书院（Merton College）为例，1264 年，该书院由 1261 年至 1263 年任英格兰大法官的瓦尔特·德·墨顿（Walter de Merton）在伦敦西南的穆尔登（Malden）所设立，为一批学者提供住宿。墨顿同时订立了书院的自治章程及明确了属于书院的产业。该书院 1274 年迁至牛津，成为牛津大学成员书院之一。墨顿本人长期从政，与皇室关系密切，擅长法律和外交，亦为教会中人，因此 1272 年至 1274 年第二度掌大法官卸任后，获委任为罗切斯特教区主教（Bishop of Rochester），直至 1277 年去世。在英国女王御准的 2015 年新修订书院章程中，其序言（preface）征引了墨顿 1274 年第三次修订书院章程时写下的序言，其中称书院为"墨顿学者之舍"（The House of the Scholars of Merton）。墨顿在序言中有时称书院为宿舍（domum, domui），有时为学校（scolis），虽没有提及 college 一词，但其性质兼具学术与住宿的功能，殆无疑问。该书院迁牛津后始称"College of Merton"，与院名"The House of the Scholars of Merton"并行。书院早期以教授神学为主，后来涉及法学、医学、人文学等。

作为神职人员，墨顿手订的章程，看来更像他以上帝之名和书院成员之间立下的誓约，规定了创办人和成员间的各种权利和义务。该章程第三十八条强调了成员责任中重中之重的，团结互助、和平、和谐慈爱（unity and mutual charity, peace, concord and love）等美德。时至今日，2015 年通过的现行书院章程，开宗明义即说书院必须为增进公众福祉（for the public benefit）而促进教育、学习、研究以及宗教。可见墨顿书院自创办七个世纪以来，一直秉承以学术谋求人类福祉的教育传统。19 世纪以来，牛津大学的课程涵盖甚广，学生入学时已经选定专业，不要求必修人文学科或博雅教育基础课程，也没有类似其他大学的机制可以系统地培养学生的品格。书院学术教育，亦以学生的主修专业为主。在这种学科主导课程的格局之下，书院生活中的同宿共膳、耳提面命、师友互动、和谐氛围、细致的书院传统礼仪、庄严典雅的教堂、气氛庄重的高桌晚宴等，无疑扮演着十分重要的潜移默化的育人角色。

Chapter 1

The Traditions in Education

范宽《溪山行旅图》
Travelers Among Mountains and Streams by Fan Kuan

There is a long history of educational institutions, both private and public, in China and in the West.

Before the Qin Dynasty, there already existed a variety of public educational institutions under different names. From the Qin and Han dynasties onwards until later the Ming and Qing dynasties, there were imperial educational establishments under the central government as well as local schools at provincial, prefectural and county levels. The imperial civil service examination system (*keju*) was first introduced in the Sui and Tang dynasties. From the Song to Qing dynasties, it became the main mechanism of recruiting officials for the government, giving rise to different levels of government-run educational institutions, where the Four Books and the Five Classics, and the orthodox teachings of Neo-Confucianism as imperial ideology were taught.

During the Spring and Autumn Period and the Warring States Period, according to the legends, Confucius gathered some 3,000 disciples who were nurtured by four subjects (virtuous conduct, speech, government, culture and learning) and six arts (rites, music, archery, chariotry, calligraphy, mathematics); while Mozi's advocacy for universal love and anti-aggression attracted hundreds of followers. Both are exemplary early non-governmental education. For a time during the Six Dynasties period, aristocratic families would set up studies at home, and Buddhist monasteries became popular venues for private learning. By the middle of the Tang Dynasty, "*shuyuan*" (academy), literally a house of books, came into being, initially referring to rooms in the house for conserving books, similar to a depository for scriptures in a Buddhist temple, then evolving to refer to an educational institution for learning. At the beginning of the Song

Dynasty, imperial civil service examinations were used more extensively for the purpose of recruitment and selection for government officials. People started pursuing studies to prepare for the exam, flocking to private institutions, such as the Yingtian Academy, many of whose students would successfully pass the imperial civil service examination and enter the officialdom. This emerging trend of private learning, advocated subsequently by prominent Confucian scholars in the Song Dynasty, led to the proliferation of academies in many major cities as well as in scenic countryside. They became the most important private educational institutions outside the government school system for nurturing literati and scholar-officials in the history of traditional education in China.

While Chinese traditional education was conducted by both government and private institutions, the two educational channels were in fact inextricably intertwined. *Shuyuan* founders, supporters, teachers and students or their family members often served in or were associated with the government. Well-known academies also received recognition through state bestowals of books and name plaques, as well as endowment of properties and land by the local government, in addition to private sponsorship. Therefore, it was impossible to dissociate these private institutions completely from the government establishment. The relationship between academies and the imperial civil service examination system also changed with time. Some continued to prepare students for taking imperial civil service examination; some devoted to pursuit in philosophical and political discourse; yet some became centres of political dissent. In the Qing Dynasty, academies resumed to serve mainly for the exam preparation, which was no different from government schools. *Shuyuan* education emphasised learning from great teachers, seeking answers to questions, studying classics, discussing and debating with one another, and cultivating moral integrity. On one hand, at academies that believed that the purpose of education is the advancement of the common good rather than attainment of power, wealth and status, classes were not confined to the preparation for the examination, so the learning environment was rather flexible — teachers taught freely in pursuit of excellence, and students came and left as they pleased. On the other hand, some academies branded their masters and their schools of thought to attract students, sometimes leading to students blindly following these masters' doctrines, forming like-minded cliques and becoming intolerant of other teachings.

All in all, traditional education in China, be it public or private, placed equal emphasis on the moral character and knowledge. The curriculum, with the core being the study of Confucian classics and moral principles such as the "three cardinal bonds (father-son, ruler-subject, husband-wife) and five constant virtues (humanity, integrity, propriety, wisdom, sincerity)", required also the mastery of both literature and history as well as general knowledge of a wide variety of subjects from the hundred schools of thought such as philosophy, mathematics, agriculture, commerce, craft and engineering. As a result, traditional intellectuals were often highly educated and widely knowledgeable. If they served in official positions, they would try to put theories into practice in governance and serving the society. If they were civilians, they would practise law or medicine, improve the community's infrastructure, build schools to promote education, and foster harmony in the community. The academies from the Song and Ming dynasties best exemplify this education tradition, as they focused on not only the study of classics in four branches of knowledge, but also the cultivation of moral character and virtues. As advocated by Zhu Xi, the Neo-Confucian master and a venerated figure in *shuyuan* education, it is believed that effective investigation of true knowledge could not be accomplished without sincerity in mind and genuine self-rectification. It goes without saying that only knowledge acquired as such would lead to self-cultivation and proper service to the country. Self-cultivation and the pursuit of knowledge should therefore be complementary to each other and the wish to contribute to the family and the society should be what motivates learning in the first place. In conclusion, traditional Chinese education emphasises both morality and knowledge, expertise and erudition. The *shuyuan* in the Song and Ming dynasties, in particular, valued especially the cultivation of the student's temperament and character as the foundation for learning.

Bailudong Academy (White Deer Cave Academy) in present Jiangxi was perhaps the most influential, while Yuelu Academy in present Hunan has continued up to the present day and still functions as a higher education institution. The treasured heritage of Bailudong Academy is its *Regulations of Bailudong Academy* (*Schools Rules of Bailudong Academy*) written by Neo-Confucian master Zhu Xi in 1179 while he was Prefect of Nankang. This text was held in esteem as a model of regulations for the *shuyuan* over the centuries. It is stated at the outset of the document that *shuyuan* education aims to impart to students the protocol and moral of the five cardinal relationships between father and son, sovereign and subject, husband

位于雅典娜林多斯面向爱琴海的多力克神庙
Doric temple, Athena, Lindos, facing Aegean Sea

and wife, elders and youngsters, and among friends. Regarding students' learning, the five stages need to be followed: to learn broadly, to examine closely, to reflect thoroughly, to judge rightly and to practice earnestly. The first four stages were aimed at full understanding of the knowledge and truths in question. Earnest practice refers to achieving oneness in knowledge and practice. There are three specific aspects to earnest practice: cultivating of oneself, handling of matters and engaging of others. For cultivating oneself, one should keep one's words sincere and truthful, take respectful and honourable actions, show restraint in anger and desires, and enhance morality and rectify wrongdoing. When handling things, one should opt for righteousness rather than scheming for profit, and manifest the highest principle without seeking merit. Finally, in one's dealings with others, do not do unto others what one would not have them do unto oneself; reflect on oneself introspectively when faced with obstacles. These exemplary principles illustrate the ultimate goal of *shuyuan* education, which is the pursuit of morality and ethics. The teaching method is centred on allowing students to fully understand and take to heart moral principles through thinking, inquiry, judgment, and practice. Moreover, having the knowledge is far from enough as it must be put into practice. There are several guidelines to be followed in practice, which correspond to the three aspects of personal cultivation, problem solving, and interaction with others respectively.

Yuelu Academy was founded in 976 by Zhu Dong, the Prefect of Tanzhou (present day Changsha), on the original site of a Buddhist temple school. When Emperor Zhenzong of the Song Dynasty summoned Zhou Shi, the Head of the *shuyuan*, and conferred the *shuyuan* a name plaque inscribed in the emperor's calligraphy, the *shuyuan* became widely known throughout the empire. During the Southern Song Dynasty, thanks to the Confucian Master Zhang Shi's teaching at the *shuyuan*, as well as his famous meeting with Zhu Xi where they discussed and debated *The Doctrine of the Mean*, the academy's reputation rose once again and came to be acclaimed as one of the four great *shuyuans*. When heading the Tanzhou government in 1194, Zhu Xi rejuvenated and expanded Yuelu Academy. He gave lectures in person during which he might have introduced his *Regulations of Bailudong Academy*. It was said that his disciples numbered as many as 1,000. In spite of the ups and downs over the three dynasties of Yuan, Ming and Qing that followed, the *shuyuan* was sustained by continual restoration by the government or individuals, and thus escaped fading into oblivion. Throughout the imperial period, Yuelu Academy persisted with its traditional education aim to cultivate scholar-officials (*shidafu*) with high moral integrity who could govern beneficently. It nurtured generations of elites of Hunan, such as Zeng Guofan, renowned for their erudition and achievements. During the education reforms in the late Qing Dynasty, the *shuyuan* was replaced by *xuetang* (schools) and the imperial civil service examinations were abolished and replaced by the Western schooling system. Yuelu Academy also evolved under different names and organisational fomrs such as Hunan Institute of Higher Learning (1903), Hunan University (1926), National Hunan University (1937) and Hunan University (1959).

In 1986, Hunan University completed the restoration of Yuelu Academy as a constituent unit of the university and it retained the name of Yuelu Academy. Within the academy, an institute of cultural studies, and the bachelor's, master's, doctoral and post-doctoral degree programmes in history, philosophy, archaeology and other disciplines were established one after another. According to the university's profile, Hunan University has inherited and carried forward the tradition of "transmission of knowledge and morality so as to benefit the people, being patriotic and pragmatic, contributing to society with practical knowledge, and being open-minded and inclusive". Its overarching goal is to nurture talents of solid foundation and broad perspective with both ability and integrity.

The Western education system can be traced back to the *paideia* education of the ancient Greek city-states. The concept of *paideia* implies a wide range of meaning including culture, civilisation, literacy, and civilising. Different from China's educational development trajectory, which evolved from a government system into a dual system of private and government schools, in the Greek city-states, the evolution is from a military education supported by the aristocracy to a non-military civil education, as exemplified by Athenian education. In earlier times, individual teachers (*didaskalos*) took on students, mainly from the nobility, and imparted knowledge and skills of sports, writing and art, in order to cultivate "gentlemanly qualities" (*kalos kagathos*) of both virtue and intelligence. After the 5th century, the school-like institution *scholés* emerged in the *paideia* system, and the scope of education was expanded to include grammar, logic, rhetoric, philosophy, ethics, oratory, debate, music, arts, arithmetic, geometry, astronomy, geography, history, politics and physical education. Among them, grammar, logic and rhetoric gradually came to form the three arts (*trivium*), which were the knowledge to be acquired by free citizens (*liberalis*) as opposed to slaves. For further learning, free citizens were expected to engage the four arts (*quadrivium*), namely astronomy, arithmetic, geometry and music. These seven arts (*ars*) constituted the main part of the liberal arts education (*ars liberalis*), which aimed to cultivate liberal citizens of virtue and intelligence who were erudite and capable of exploring the truth of the universe and life. The liberal arts education was also known as *enkuklios paideia*, referring to whole-person education or holistic education, where *enkuklios* bore meanings of well-rounded, circular, general, common, etc. Some of these *scholés* evolved into famous educational institutions, for exploring knowledge, debating the

truth, and as a repository of books and literature, as was the case with the Academy established by Plato and the Lyceum by Aristotle. This kind of Roman-Hellenistic education was later provided throughout the Roman empire, often with official funding. The curricula carried on the Hellenistic *paideia* tradition, emphasising humanities (*humanitas*) and usually covered liberal arts education as represented by the seven arts. It also incorporated the Roman legal tradition dating back to the times of *The Law of the Twelve Tables* (*Duodecim Tabulae*) of the 5th century BC. The purpose of the Roman humanistic education was likewise to nurture liberal Roman citizens with both intelligence and virtue.

The decline of the Western Roman Empire in the 5th century marked the beginning of the Middle Ages. Early in this period, the principal centres of learning shifted to Christian monasteries. By transcribing ancient texts, monks were trained to be proficient in the Greek and Roman classics and in the interpretation of the Bible, and they were also cultivated to uphold the Christian ethics of nobility and chastity, compassion and charity. After hundreds of years punctuated by wars, from the city-states, principalities and kingdoms, which claimed to rule locally or regionally, to the Holy Roman Empire and Roman Catholic Church, which claimed to overrule the entire Western world, all formed their respective political and social systems of authority. In this plethora of power regimes, various educational institutions sprang up to cater to the different needs in their respective territories. There were local government schools, church-run schools, professional guilds, private schools brought together and run by students and teachers, etc. After the 12th century, a higher education system called university (*universitas*) came into being, which was an epoch-making development in the history of Western education and established the basic model of Western higher education. With an immeasurable impact that lasts to the present time, it has become the globally adopted system of higher education.

The defining features of a university is that of a statutory association of professors and/ or students in a particular community, recognised and authorised by the ruling powers or by the Papacy, to impart academic knowledge, to confer degrees to those who passed the statutory examinations, and to administer its affairs in accordance with its own charter and statutes. On one hand, universities tend to remain in their place of establishment, and thus often take their location to be their namesake. Students and teachers, on the other hand, came from all corners of Europe yet enjoyed all the legal privileges and rights as the local residents. The education would be almost entirely unrelated to local matters, focusing instead on issues of general or universal significance such as humanities, theology, jurisprudence and medicine, following the Greco-Roman education tradition that preceded it. The awarded degree would be widely recognised and graduates could teach in schools or pursue their qualified profession throughout Europe; the universities with early success were therefore open and universal. The most famous ones were the University of Bologna, the University of Paris and the University of Oxford. The former is believed to be the first university in Europe, claimed to be founded in 1188. Although the founding date is in dispute, certainly, by the early 13th century, the University of Bologna undoubtedly had the characteristics of what constitutes a university in our understanding, with its main focus on legal education and jurisprudence. Established from religious schools of the 11th and 12th centuries, the University of Paris and the University of Oxford also evolved to become universities in the early 13th century. The universities comprised the Faculty of Arts (*Facultatis Artium*) as the foundation level of learning, and three superior faculties, namely, the Faculty of Theology, the Faculty of Law and the Faculty of Medicine, for further education. Among these faculties, the Faculty of Theology was the most prestigious one. In the early 13th century, a group of professors from the University of Oxford moved to Cambridge and built another university, thus named as the University of Cambridge. With a similar structure, it became a university on a par with the University of Oxford. Among the four early faculties of Cambridge, the Faculty of Theology and its affiliated philosophy degree were initially among its strengths.

As with the University of Paris, when the University of Oxford and the University of Cambridge were being established in the early 13th century, the need for a mechanism to arrange accommodation for students and teachers arose. This was because the majority of students and professors were non-locals, and the renting of accommodation from local residents sometimes led to feuds and even violence and casualties. This need led to the creation of a type of educational institution that was a constituent of the university but had its own independent governance and assets. Some such lodgings were named as a hall, or house, and latterly others were named as a college. Hall is an Old English word for guest house, derived from *hospitium* in Latin; House, or *domum* in Latin, meant a house in general. Both terms evolved into a form of statutory educational accommodation for professors and students. As for college, for which *collegium* in Latin, it originally

meant a corporation with legal status. All three evolved into a form of statutory educational accommodation for professors and students alike. At the University of Oxford and the University of Cambridge, the names college, house and hall were officially translated into Chinese as "学院" (*xueyuan*), a Chinese term in use to mean a disciplinary-based academic faculty of a university in modern Chinese. In Chinese literature on the history of Western education, college, house and hall are sometimes translated as "学舍"(*xueshe*). When discussing the college system at the University of Oxford and the University of Cambridge, the Chinese academic community often refers to it as the "书院" (*shuyuan*), as distinguished from "学院" (*faculty*). To avoid confusion, this book adopts the more widely used term of "书院" (*shuyuan*) as the translation of "college" in the Oxbridge context. These university-affiliated colleges were able to attract well-educated and reputable scholars from all over Europe, as they provided accommodations and various statutory privileges for the residential professors. The colleges' educational role was no less important than that of the university's faculties and their affiliated departments, and they offered academic subjects on humanities, law, medicine and theology just as those taught in the faculties. However, as professors and students shared communal meals, studied and lived together at the college, professors were able to interact more closely with their students and teach them by example, which has an educational impact that cannot be achieved through lectures at faculties. Of course, college professors were often employed by faculties at the same time, and students, apart from being taught by professors affiliated to their own college, were also taught in faculties by professors affiliated with other colleges. From the perspective of discipline-specific education, colleges and faculties each has its own role to play, but they achieved synergy by complementing and supplementing each other. Nevertheless, the authority to examine outcome of learning and award degrees accordingly, both of which constitute key functions of a university, remained within the purview of the university and faculties. Colleges had the responsibility to educate but not the right to confer degrees.

For instance, Merton College, one of the three oldest colleges in the University of Oxford, was founded in 1264 by Walter de Merton, after his first term as Lord Chancellor of England from 1261 to 1263, on his private property in Malden, to the southwest of London, to provide accommodation for a group of scholars. The founder, who was close to the royal family, prominent in law and diplomacy, and influential as a clergyman, also provisioned land and property and established a charter of self-governance for the new institution. In 1274, after Merton's second term as Lord Chancellor from 1272—1274, it was moved to Oxford, acquired another name of Merton College, and became one of the university's constituent colleges. Merton was appointed Bishop of Rochester in the same year until his death in 1277. In the 3rd revised statutes of the college of 1274 drawn up by Merton, which named the institution as "The House of the Scholars of Merton" (*domum scolarium de Merton*) and referred to the institution alternatingly as a dormitory (*domum, domui*), and a school (*scolis*) in the preamble. Although the word "college" is not mentioned in this 1274 charter, there is no doubt that the institution was both academic and residential in nature, and thus a genuine college. The name "College of Merton" came into existence after the move to Oxford, and it co-existed alongside the original name "The House of the Scholars of Merton". During the early years, theology was the main focus of the college, but later it also offered subjects in law, medicine and humanities. The statutes drawn up by Merton, him being a clergyman, resembled an oath in the name of God between him the founder and the college members, stipulating their respective rights and duties. Article 38 particularly emphasised the virtues of unity and mutual charity, peace, concord and love as the most important of the duties. Today, the current statutes of the college, which were adopted in 2015 state at the outset that the college must advance education, learning, research and religion "for the public benefit". It is evident that in the seven centuries since its establishment, Merton College has upheld a tradition of pursuing the betterment of mankind through academic pursuit.

Since the 19th century, the University of Oxford has offered a broad curriculum, yet each student enrolling into a particular course (major subject), with no requirements in compulsory foundational studies in humanities or liberal arts education. Nor was there a university mechanism for systematically moulding the character of the students. The academic education of the colleges mainly focused on the students' chosen subjects. Under this discipline-oriented curriculum, the communal meals and shared living spaces, the earnest advice, the interaction between professors and students, the contagious atmosphere of intellectual inquiry, the peer earning experience, the elaborate rituals and traditions of the college, the stately and elegant chapel and the solemn formal dinners, all undoubtedly played a very important role in the subtle nurturing of students' character in addition to acquisition of knowledge.

第二章

现代中西住宿式书院的发展

前一章论述的中西书院教育传统，均具有提供学生住宿的特点。张栻的《宋岳麓书院记》记载了976年岳麓书院创立时，即有"以待四方学者"的宗旨，故建筑必包括住宿之所。朱熹在《潭州委教授措置岳麓书院牒》中提及斋舍、几案、床榻等住宿设施。英国墨顿学院1264年创立时，亦旨在为外地而来的学者提供学舍。故此中西书院皆具有住宿式书院的功能。

虽继承了英国牛剑（Oxbridge）式的传统书院，但又另辟蹊径的是17世纪、18世纪流行于北美殖民地的独立文理学院（independent liberal arts college），最重要的莫如1636年成立而三年后取名为哈佛的哈佛学院（Harvard College）、1701年成立的耶鲁学院（Yale College）以及1746年成立的新泽西学院（College of New Jersey）。新泽西学院1896年改名为普林斯顿大学。三家学院，早年均以包含文科及理科的西方传统博雅教育为主，故有文理学院之称。哈佛和耶鲁后来不断发展，陆续增加了研究院，以及各种各样实用型专门学院（professional schools）如神学院、法学院、医学院等，渐成19世纪、20世纪的综合型研究大学，原来的文理学院则不再独立，而成为本科生学术管理单位。时至今日，两所大学的本科生，仍在管理本科生的文理学院注册，沿用哈佛学院及耶鲁学院的体制，但上课则在文理科学院（Faculty of Arts and Sciences）。后者统筹各主修专业和学院，推动研究，亦为不属于文理学院的研究生提供研究院教育。两校博雅教育的人文传统仅适用于本科生，体现在必修的通识课程上。普林斯顿大学更加强调本科的博雅教育传统，除强调高层次的基础研究之外，没有如哈佛、耶鲁般建立了庞大的研究生院，没有法学院、医学院等实用型专门学院。

这三所美国顶尖大学，反映了今天美国本科高等教育的两大类型。一是综合式的大学，本科教育虽教授主修科目的专业知识，但非常强调通识教育，其往往在课程中占相当大的比重，借以传承博雅教育的人文传统。二是以博雅教育为主导的小班教学和以本科教育为主的独立文理学院。前者是主流，数以千计。后者亦以百计。在美国，媒体公认的国家级别的大学（national universities）有300多所，国家级别的独立文理学院（national liberal arts colleges）亦有200所左右。哈佛、耶鲁无疑属于前者，普林斯顿大学虽不在文理学院之列，但其本科教育则更像后者。

西方以博雅教育为主的大学教育兴起以来，包括牛剑式书院及美国的文理学院，一直以培育学识通博、道德高尚的优秀神职人员、公仆、学者等通才社会领袖为己任，学生亦多具精英背景。这个传统，百多年来在现代社会洗礼之下，开始面临各种挑战。首先，1810年柏林大学成立，首倡大学的科研使命，学术研究渐渐成为各地大学所向往的。柏林大学原意是将研究与育人融合为一，但后来发现这个理想不易落实。著名的1828年《耶鲁报告》，正反映了当时对还要不要把包括希腊文和拉丁文在内的古典人文学作为博雅教育核心课程的争议。其次，19世纪中叶以来，社会达尔文主义、实证主义、科学主义、现实主义、价值中立的社会科学、唯市场主义、后现代主义等思潮，次第成为大学校园的显学，使得道德相对主义广泛流行，学术知识与道德品格不再作为一贯的教育成果，与博雅教育的德育理念扞格不入。最后，20世纪初以来，大学教育逐渐向社会开放，越来越大众化的结果，给普通学生带来就业压力，导致原来以小班教学为主及反就业导向的为精英学生开设的博雅教育机构亦不得不开始考虑来自现实社会的压力。20 世纪中叶以来，科技研究更渐渐与教育人才分道扬镳，并且往往取代后者成为大学的首要之务。凡此种种，皆与博雅育人之宗旨大相径庭。

虽然如此，20 世纪后期高等教育同时又变得越来越重视学生的德育。这种逆转的原因不一，或因校友言行举止为社会所不齿，则不论在科研或政经领域如何卓越突出，终究为母校留下难以磨灭的污点；或因 20 世纪后期高等教育中素质问责保证流行，而学生品格往往成为检验教育结果的重要指标；或因大学课程日趋以就业为导向，亦不能不顾及未来雇主对学生的人品要求，而雇主对大学生品格的要求，往往大于其专业知识；与此同时，与其他营利或非营利的企业机构无异，大学亦必须承担更多的社会责任，培育学生的品格顺理成章地成为大学责无旁贷的义务，因此大学更不能置学生品格培育于不顾，而只专注于科研。

上述种种，都在博雅教育传统理想与现代大学教育现实之间，造成了高度的张力，促使部分大学开始探索如何在两者之间取得平衡。在各种解决范式之中，住宿式书院制度无疑成为具有吸引力的方案。

住宿式书院（residential college）在英美有各种各样的模式，但与一般仅供学生起居的宿舍相比，除同样具有住宿设施之外，必定有相异之处。关键是一般住宿式书院在大学教育中扮演了不同程度的机构角色。这种角色主要针对品格培育，但也可以包括学术方面的培育。此外，住宿式书院更强调同宿共膳和书院社群的教化作用。这种教育理念和制度，固然源自牛剑式书院，但在学术专科教育上，没有扮演牛剑式书院般重要的角色；同时，其因为附属于大学而非独立实体，所以并非牛剑式书院的翻版。住宿式书院在过去二十年随着高等教育全球化而遍及世界各地，方兴未艾，更有人称为"住宿式书院运动"。究其源起，可以上溯至 20 世纪 30 年代的哈佛大学和耶鲁大学。

20 世纪初，阿伯特·劳伦斯·洛厄尔（Abbott Lawrence Lowell）任职哈佛大学校长后，不断倡议设立新的校内学生住宿单位，以期创造不同社会背景学生得以融合互动的社群条件，打破当时贫富分化且关系日益疏离的学生住宿状况，让学识与志趣千差万别的师生同宿共膳，相互切磋，激发求知欲，刺激思考，从而栽培思想有深度及有责任感的人民与社会领袖，避免产生擅长专业知识却牟利进取、偏见狭隘、罔顾公益的自私自利之徒，但这种育人的理念遇到许多阻力。幸而耶鲁校友石油业巨子爱德华·哈克尼斯（Edward Harkness）因耶鲁不积极支持洛厄尔设立类似牛剑式书院的请求，转而捐赠哈佛大学上千万美元，希望玉成其事。洛厄尔遂得以排除障碍而建立起哈佛大学的"学舍"制度。前述牛津大学墨顿书院章程内，学院名称除 college 外，也可用 house 等，故此哈佛的学舍被称为 house，仍不脱牛剑式书院的传统。1930 年，两个学舍落成，命名为邓斯特学舍（Dunster House）及洛厄尔学舍（Lowell House）。学舍制至今仍为哈佛所强调的"本科生大学经验的基础"（foundation of the undergraduate experience at Harvard College）。哈佛大学共有十二个学舍，专为二年级以上的本科生而设。一年级学生则住在哈佛园（Harvard Yard）内或周边的宿舍（dormitories），一般称 hall 或 court。

1925 年，耶鲁大学校长詹姆斯·罗兰·安吉尔（James Rowland Angell）建议建立住宿式书院制，仿牛剑式书院设立一批住宿式书院，以解决学生人数增加导致宿位不足以及人际关系疏离，难以培育理想人才的困境。虽得到同样推崇牛剑式书院的校友哈克尼斯的捐款承诺，但久久未能落实。哈佛大学获哈克尼斯捐赠而启动学舍计划后，耶鲁大学始再续前议，后获哈克尼斯赠予近 1600 万美元，启动校园加建住宿式书院计划。1933 年落成七间书院；至 1940 年陆续增加三间；至今耶鲁共有住宿式书院十四间。初期住宿式书院仅供二年级以上本科生居住；1962 年起，所有一年级学生随机派到各住宿式书院。住宿式书院制至今亦成为耶鲁"本科生经验的核心所在"（at the heart of the Yale experience）。

哈佛大学、耶鲁大学的学舍或住宿式书院，均仿自牛剑式书院，强调学舍或住宿式书院师生通过同宿共膳、朝夕相处，建立学习社群，兼容共济，相互切磋，互相支持，以期达到潜移默化、修养品格的教化之效。但亦有较大的差异。哈佛大学和耶鲁大学的学舍或住宿式书院除并非独立实体之外，亦非专业学科的授受之所。学舍或住宿式书院中驻院或不驻院学术人员、研究生或高年级学生，除照顾及指导学生校园生活和与个人成长有关的各种问题外，亦从事一般的学术辅导工作，如解决学习问题、主修和选修科目的选择、学术生涯规划等，但学术辅导的内容与主修专业的学术教育，不一定有直接关系。牛剑式书院提供的专门学术教育，与颁授学位的学院同步进行，没有其他通识教育课程。哈佛大学、耶鲁大学的本科阶段虽有学术教育，但专业以外的通识教育要求涵盖了基本的学术范畴。哈佛大学以通识教育（general education）为主导；耶鲁大学以选修课为主导（distributional requirements），此外学生自选科目的空间颇大，可在前两年广泛修读不同学科之后，大三、大四才选择主修专业。耶鲁明言本科教育着重培养智慧智能与博学通才，不过于传授主修科目的既定知识。在这种让学生自由追求学术兴趣的环境之下，哈佛大学和耶鲁大学的学舍和住宿式书院的多元学术环境以及开放而非专科性的学术辅导，无疑较牛剑式书院的专业专科辅导更为恰当。

与哈佛大学、耶鲁大学相比，由1746年成立的新泽西文理学院演变而成的普林斯顿大学，虽然是顶尖的研究型大学之一，但保留了更多的文理学院博雅教育传统。其教育宗旨特别强调"服务人类"（in service of humanity）；在校园内为徽碑的非正式校训要求大学以"服务国家，服务人类"（Princeton in the nation's service and the service of humanity）为本。普林斯顿以博雅教育为大学核心使命价值，以此开阔学生眼界，塑造学生的品格和价值观，鼓励学生探索人文、艺术、科学、工程及社会科学的理念及方法，磨炼阅写技巧以及全面的思维，作为毕生事业成就的基石，借以承担社会领袖之责，服务国家及全人类，并得以追求以公益为先的有意义人生。为更有效地达到这种育人目的，普林斯顿自20世纪80年代起，次第成立了六家全面实行住宿式书院制度的书院，均融合共膳、社群及学术辅导功能于一身。普林斯顿大学认为住宿式

书院的社群凝聚力，对学生确立诚实、廉洁、公平等基本价值观至关重要。同时，较诸哈佛、耶鲁，普林斯顿住宿式书院的学术主任（dean）及学业主任（director of studies）负有督导院生学业进度的职责，即更强调学术与育人的结合。这些住宿式书院现已成为普林斯顿大学最重要的特色之一。所有一年级学生，均派到住宿式书院，三年级时始可选择其他居所。由此可见，普林斯顿的本科博雅教育，特别强调通过住宿式书院，培育学生的品格素养，作为立德立业之本。

20世纪是中国高等教育全面西化的时期。胡适1923年发表题为《书院制史略》的演讲，慨叹晚清废书院为西式学堂，实属一大不幸，因为此举断送了千年来中国学者刻苦研究与自由思考的书院精神。他的出发点在比附传统书院与当时西方流行的道尔顿学制，他对传统书院的理解全面与否可容商榷，但足以说明传统书院在20世纪的中国曾经变成被淘汰的"古迹"。

20世纪50年代起，陆续有私人办学而以书院命名的小型文理学院出现，例如香港的新亚书院。开始时师生人数很少，在租赁的楼房里同宿共膳，传授学业。创院时仿宋明书院订立学规，共二十四条。开宗明义的五条说："一、求学与做人，贵能齐头并进，更贵能融通合一。二、做人的最高基础在求学，求学之最高旨趣在做人。三、爱家庭、爱师友、爱国家、爱民族、爱人类，为求学做人之中心基点。对人类文化有了解，对社会事业有贡献，为求学做人之向往目标。四、祛除小我功利计算，打破专为谋职业、谋资历而进学校之浅薄观念。五、职业仅为个人，事业则为大众。立志成功事业，不怕没有职业，专心谋求职业，不一定能成事业。"可谓传统书院教育理想的现代化例子之一。其后受耶鲁大学雅礼协会资助，该校始得建立校舍。1963年该校与崇基学院及联合书院组成香港中文大学，变成新大学成员书院之一。时至今日，作为一种特别重视品格教化作用的高等教育机构，各种各样的高等教育书院已经如雨后春笋，在中国各地流行起来。

作为大学教育组成元素的住宿式书院制度，21世纪开始亦受到中国高等教育界的重视。这里仅举2006年成立的香港中文大学善衡书院以及2005年启动的复旦大学复旦学院与其住宿书院为例，说明中国住宿式书院制度的育人特色。

香港中文大学1963年由崇基、新亚、联合三所文理学院联合组成。自1976年起，三间成员书院的文理学院式学术功能，转移到大学本部的文、理、商、工、教等各专业学院。成员书院继续照顾学生生活、管理宿舍之外，并负担部分通识教育的功能。由于学生人数增加，1986年又成立了逸夫书院。2012年香港公立大学学制由三年改为四年，香港中文大学再增添五个书院，全校住宿学生增加一半以上，其中部分书院更成为本科四年全程住宿书院，善衡书院即其中之一，各级学生共600名。书院除具有生活功能及提供课外活动，仍提供两门共六学分书院通识课程，占全部通识教育学分的四分之一，借以承载书院的教育理念及传统，帮助同学在学术追求以外全面发展，成为现今世界尽责的公民。善衡书院的院训为"文、行、忠、信"，教育愿景是培育学生的"文化素养、高尚情操、社会责任感及诚信的品德"。书院两大教育理念是使书院成为亲切的"家"以及提供课堂外学习的机会。后者或被教育界称为第二课堂。

复旦大学2005年成立复旦学院，作为学校实施通识教育的教学、研究和管理机构，负责全校本科一年级和部分二年级学生教育教学管理工作，同时借鉴国外大学住宿式书院的做法，承续中国书院文化传统。在复旦学院之下，又成立了志德、腾飞、克卿、任重四间书院，以"读书、修身"为核心价值，兼顾"转变、关爱"。书院制与导师制相结合，辅以通识核心课程，全面推动通识教育。一年级学生不分院系入住各书院，一同生活及学习。各书院均以复旦先贤命名，而住宿楼"既是学生生活空间，更是学生交流学业思想、切磋人生体悟、培养集体意识、提升精神境界的空间"。"每一位新同学经过在复旦学院一年的学习生活，树立远大志向，夯筑宽厚学养，塑造完善人格，陶冶复旦精神，并为后三年的专业学习和全面发展打好基础。"2012年宣布重组的新复旦学院为本科生院，前一年成立的希德书院加入组成复旦学院下属的五间"贯穿本科

教育的住宿书院"。书院亦相应改革，由管理实体转型为功能虚体；由全面负责学生管理、学习、修身工作，改为负责促进学生全面发展的第二课堂育人工作；由负责一年级学生的奠基教育，变为负责贯穿本科全过程的育人教育。复旦大学的人才培养目标是"以培养德智体美劳全面发展的社会主义建设者和接班人为根本，坚持国家意识、人文情怀、科学精神、专业素养、国际视野的育人特色，为国家兴旺、社会发展、人类文明进步培养更多领袖人才、行业栋梁及社会英才，培养担当民族复兴大任、掌握未来的复旦人"。各书院学生的专业集中于一些大类，如腾飞书院以工程技术院系学生为主，任重书院以文学、管理等院系学生为主，希德书院则以物理学、化学院系学生为主等。

住宿式书院在中国如雨后春笋般出现，方兴未艾。2014年"首届高校现代书院制教育论坛"在北京航空航天大学举行，并成立高校书院联盟。至2021年先后举办论坛七次，出席学者数以千计，来自百所以上高校，出版论文集五种。总体来说，有关住宿式书院的中文研究，成果不断涌现，课题日益深入，水平快速提升。虽然对于具体制度设计以及资源投放，各校千差万别，但其共通之处是认同大学在传授及创造知识之外，还必须培育学生品格。在此基础之上，大家都不得不接受这样一个前提，即住宿式书院，或许是目前培育学生品格最有效的大学教育机制之一。

香港中文大学善衡书院"家"字艺术雕塑
The Sculpture of HOME, S.H. Ho College of the Chinese University of Hong Kong

Chapter 2

Development of Modern Chinese and Western Residential Colleges

The previous chapter described the college traditions in China and the West, both of which incorporated elements of residential accommodation for students. According to Zhang Shi's *Narration of Yuelu Academy in the Song Dynasty*, when the *shuyuan* was founded in 976, it already had the aim of "welcoming scholars from all directions". It clearly implies that its buildings must have included lodgings. Zhu Xi's *Note on the Teaching Commission and Arrangements for Yuelu Academy in Tanzhou* mentioned boarding facilities such as dormitories, desks, and beds. When it was first established in 1264, Merton College also intended to provide on-campus residence for scholars from abroad. In other words, both originally intended to function as residential colleges.

Inheriting the tradition of Oxbridge colleges in England yet taking a different approach were the independent liberal arts colleges that became popular in the 17th and 18th centuries in the North American colonies. The most important of these was Harvard College, approved by the Great and General Court of the Governor and Company of the Massachusetts Bay in New England to be established in 1636 and officially named after John Harvard three years later; Yale College, founded by an act passed by Governor and General Assembly of the Connecticut Colony in 1701 and named after Elihu Yale in 1718; and the College of New Jersey, chartered in 1746 and renamed Princeton University in 1896. In the early years, the three colleges focused on traditional liberal arts education, encompassing humanities and scientific education, therefore, they were known as liberal arts colleges. By the 19th and 20th centuries, Harvard and Yale had developed into comprehensive research universities, with the addition of graduate schools and a variety of professional schools such as the divinity school, the law school and the medical school. The formerly independent liberal arts colleges were no longer independent and became an academic management unit for undergraduate studies under the university. Nowadays, undergraduate students at both

universities are still registered with Harvard College and Yale College, which oversee undergraduate education, but they attend classes in the universities' Faculty of Arts and Sciences. The latter co-ordinates concentrations or major programmes within and across departments, promotes research, and also provides education for postgraduate students, who are not part of the liberal arts college. The liberal arts and humanities tradition of the two universities applies only to undergraduate students and is embodied by the compulsory general education programme and distribution requirements. Princeton University has had a particularly strong emphasis on traditional liberal arts education at the undergraduate level; while the university focuses on high-end fundamental research, it does not have large graduate schools like Harvard and Yale nor professional schools in practical areas such as law and medicine.

These three top universities in the US represent the two main categories of undergraduate educational institutions in that country today. Within the first category of comprehensive universities, while undergraduate education provides training in the major subject areas of expertise, there is also a strong emphasis on general education, which often takes up a significant proportion of the curriculum, in keeping with the humanistic tradition of liberal arts education. The other category comprises independent liberal arts colleges which focus mainly on undergraduate studies and are characterised by small-sized classes oriented towards liberal arts education. The former category makes up the mainstream, with such universities numbering in the thousands, while the latter category numbers in the hundreds. It is widely recognised that there are more than 300 national universities and 200 national liberal arts colleges in the US. While Harvard and Yale are undoubtedly in the former category, Princeton, though not considered a liberal arts college, resembles one in its undergraduate education.

Since the rise of liberal arts university education in the

West, including the colleges at Oxford and Cambridge and the liberal arts colleges in the United States, the mission was always to nurture well-educated, morally upright clergymen, public servants, scholars and other well-rounded community leaders, with many students coming from elite backgrounds. Under modernising influences for over a century, this tradition began to face various challenges. Firstly, in 1810, the University of Berlin was founded with the pioneering mission to advance scientific research, causing academic research to gradually become an aspirational vision for universities everywhere. The original intention of the University of Berlin was to integrate research and education; however, this was not easy to achieve. The famous *Yale Report* of 1828 reflected the fact that whether to retain classical humanities including Greek and Latin as the core curriculum for liberal arts education by that time become a debatable educational issue. Secondly, since the middle of the 19th century, social Darwinism, positivism, scientism, realism, value-neutral social sciences, marketism, post-modernism and other trends successively became the dominant schools of thought in university campuses. This in turn gave rise to widespread moral relativism. Academic knowledge and moral character were no longer coherent educational outcomes and this line of thinking became incompatible with the moral philosophy of liberal arts education. Furthermore, the gradually increasing access to a university education for the wider populace of society since the beginning of the 20th century resulted in pressure on the student population vis-à-vis finding employment. As a result, liberal arts institutions for elite students, which were originally centred around small-size classes and not career-oriented, had to take into account pressures from the new zeitgeist. Since the mid-20th century, scientific research has gradually detached itself from education, and has often replaced the latter as a priority for universities. All of these are incompatible with the mission of liberal arts education.

Nevertheless, from the latter part of the 20th century, higher education sector worldwide became increasingly concerned about students' moral education. This reversal was caused by various factors including the stigma attached to outrageous misconducts or crimes committed by alumni, which could leave a stain on their alma mater, irrespective of how outstanding they might be in research or in politics and economic endeavours. Another possible factor was the popularity of quality assurance and accountability in higher education in the late 20th century; student's character quality often constitutes an important education outcome. Or perhaps, despite

university courses becoming increasingly career-oriented, they could not help but take into account the character requirements of prospective employers, who often value character traits over knowledge learned at university. At the same time, like other profit-making or non-profit-making enterprises, public and private alike, universities also had to assume greater social responsibility. Therefore, it was only logical that nurturing the character of students became a moral obligation for universities. They could not focus only on scientific research and knowledge transmission but neglect the cultivation of students' moral competency.

All the above developments mean that the traditional ideal of liberal arts education must confront with the harsh reality of modern university education, resulting in a high degree of tension, and prompting some universities to explore how to strike a balance between the two. Among the various solutions, the residential college system is undoubtedly a long-established and attractive option.

While models of residential colleges in the UK and the US diverge, they are fundamentally different from the conventional dormitories that function only as living quarters for students. The crucial difference here is that residential colleges generally simultaneously play an institutional role in university education to various degrees. This role is primarily focused on character development but can also include academic learning. In addition, residential colleges emphasise the importance of communal dining and accommodation and the edifying role of the college community. While this educational philosophy and system is derived from the Oxbridge tradition, residential colleges elsewhere do not normally play the same role in terms of academic and professional education as at Oxbridge; they are not the latter's replica because many such colleges are units within the university and are not independent legal entities like Oxbridge colleges. Over the past 20 years, residential colleges have proliferated around the world in line with the globalisation of higher education, and have gained increasing popularity, with enthusiasts calling it the "residential college movement". Their origins can be traced back to Harvard and Yale of the 1930s.

In the early 20th century, Abbott Lawrence Lowell, President of Harvard University, advocated the creation of new student housing units on campus. The intent was to create conditions for students from different social backgrounds to mingle and interact with each other and break the growing separation between rich and poor in students' living environs. It was intended as a means to allow students and professors with a diverse background of knowledge and interests to share accommodation and meals, thereby stimulating intellectual curiosity and thinking, as a means to nurture thoughtful and responsible civil and social leaders, instead of knowledgeable professionals or profiteers who were narrow-minded and self-serving. However, this philosophy of education was met with much resistance. Fortunately, Edward Harkness, a Yale alumnus and an oil tycoon, who proposed to establish a college at Yale similar to Oxbridge but failed to gain full support on Yale's part, donated instead over 10 million dollars to Harvard in the hope of realising his vision in higher education. And thus, Lowell was able to overcome the obstacles and establish the Harvard house system. In the aforementioned Statutes of Merton College in Oxford, the word "house" was used in its name, in addition to "college". By donning the "house" designation, the new Harvard Houses made a linkage with Oxbridge colleges. The first two houses were completed in 1930 and named Dunster House and Lowell House. The house system has since become the foundation of the undergraduate experience at Harvard college, with 12 houses dedicated to accommodating undergraduates in their second year and above. First-year students are housed in dormitories, commonly known as halls or courts, in or around Harvard Yard.

In 1925, James Rowland Angell, President of Yale University called for the establishment of a residential college system, modelled after Oxbridge, to address the difficulties in cultivating ideal talents, caused by housing shortages and the lack of interpersonal interaction resulting from the increase in student numbers. However, despite the promise of a donation from alumnus Edward Harkness, who also advocated the Oxbridge college system, the university was not able to implement it for a long time. After Harvard received a donation from Harkness to start the house system, Yale pressed on with its initiative and received a donation of nearly 16 million dollars from Harkness to start the project to build residential colleges on campus. Seven colleges were completed in 1933, and three more were added by 1940. Presently, there are 14 residential colleges at Yale. Initially, the residential colleges were intended for undergraduate students in their second year and above. From 1962 onwards, all first-year students came to be randomly assigned to the residential colleges. The residential college system has since remained "at the heart of the Yale experience".

The houses or residential colleges at Harvard and Yale, modelled after the Oxbridge College system, emphasise the importance of professors and students sharing

accommodation and meals in order to build an inclusive learning community and provide mutual support for each other. This was with a view to achieving the effect of steadily and progressively cultivating students' character. There are important differences with Oxbridge, however, in that the houses or colleges at Harvard and Yale are not independent entities, nor are they a place where specialised disciplines are taught. Resident or non-resident academic staff, postgraduates or senior students of the house or the residential college are responsible for providing guidance for students on various aspects of campus life and personal development, as well as general academic counselling. This includes helping with learning difficulties, choice of majors and elective subjects, and academic career planning. Nonetheless, the content of academic counselling is not necessarily related to the academic subject content of a given concentration or major. Oxbridge colleges provide subject-specific academic education that run parallel to degree-awarding faculties, and have no general education programmes. While Harvard and Yale have majors at the undergraduate level, the general education requirement beyond the area of specialisation covers a wide range of basic academic areas. Harvard achieves this via its general education courses and Yale via its distributional requirements. This, together with the considerable space for other electives allows students to choose a major in the third and fourth years after studying a wide range of subjects in the first two years. Yale, for instance, states that its undergraduate education "aims to cultivate a broadly informed, highly disciplined intellect," enabling a student to "think critically and creatively in a variety of ways", far more than to focus on the transfer of established knowledge in the major disciplines. In this context, where students are encouraged to pursue their academic interests freely, the diverse academic environment of Harvard and Yale's residential colleges and their open, non-specialised academic nurturing are undoubtedly more appropriate than the subject-specific academic guidance at Oxbridge.

In contrast to Harvard and Yale, Princeton University, which evolved from the College of New Jersey founded in 1746, is one of the top research universities but retains more of the liberal arts tradition of the liberal arts colleges. The university's educational aims place particular emphasis on being "in service of humanity". The informal motto of the university, which is carved into a stone medallion on its campus, declares the commitment of "Princeton in the nation's service and the service of humanity". Princeton places liberal arts education at the heart of the university's mission, broadening students' horizons and shaping their character and values. Students are encouraged to explore ideas and methods in the humanities, arts, sciences, engineering and social sciences, to hone their reading and writing skills and to think holistically. These are considered the cornerstones of a successful career, so that graduates can assume responsibility as leaders in society, to serve their country and humanity, and to pursue a meaningful life that puts common good first. To achieve these educational goals more effectively, Princeton has established six residential colleges since the 1980s, each of which combines communal dining, living with community, and academic guidance. The university believes that the social bonds and cohesiveness of residential colleges are essential to engendering in students in the fundamental values of honesty, integrity and fairness. The dean and the director of studies at Princeton's residential colleges are responsible for overseeing the academic progress of the students, placing greater emphasis on the integration of academics and personal development than Harvard or Yale. These residential colleges now constitute one of Princeton's most important features. All first-year students are assigned to residential colleges and may choose alternative accommodation from the third year onwards. Princeton's undergraduate liberal arts education explicitly emphasises nurturing the character of its students through residential colleges as the foundation of their moral and professional development.

The 20th century saw the complete westernisation of Chinese higher education. In 1923, Hu Shi delivered a speech entitled *A Brief History of the Shuyuan System*, in which he lamented that the decision to substitute the traditional Chinese *shuyuan* in the late Qing Dynasty with Western-style education system was unfortunate, for it had discontinued the tradition of *shuyuan*, which had been a wellspring of research and free thinking for Chinese scholars for over a thousand years. His premise was the comparison between the traditional Chinese academies and the then fashionable Dalton system of education. While one may argue with his interpretation of the traditional *shuyuan*, his speech clearly indicated the fact that traditional *shuyuan* as an education system had become obsolete in 20th-century China.

Private liberal arts colleges sprang up in Hong Kong in the 1950s. One of them was the New Asia College. At the beginning, it had very few faculty members and students. Teachers shared accommodation and meals with students in a rented flat and shared their knowledge with them in a communal setting. At its

founding the college established a set of 24 rules modelled after those of the Song and Ming *shuyuans*, the leading five articles being: " (a) It is imperative to pursue knowledge and become a good person at the same time. Better still if the two endeavours are fully integrated. (b) The most solid foundation of becoming a good person lies in successful pursuit of knowledge; the highest aspiration of pursuing knowledge is to become a good person. (c) The foundation core of both pursuing knowledge and becoming good is the love of ones' family, teachers, friends, country, nation, and humankind. The ultimate aspiration behind pursuing knowledge and becoming good is to comprehend human cultures as well as to contribute to social advancement. (d) Abandon self-interested calculations, and reject the shallow notion that schooling is just for seeking employment. (e) A job is for oneself, but a career is for the people. Aspiring to serve others, one will naturally have a job; focussing on job search, one may not build a real career". These articles may reflect an example of aspiration to revive the educational ideal traditional *shuyuan*. The construction of New Asia's premise started only subsequently with funding from Yale-China Association. In 1963, together with Chung Chi College and United College, it became one of the three constituent colleges to form The Chinese University of Hong Kong (CUHK). In recent decades, college modelling on traditional *shuyuan*, with emphasis on character cultivation, has become a popular mode of high education proliferating across China.

As an integral part of university education, the residential college system has also received attention from the higher education sector in China since the turn of the century. Here we mention two examples — the fully residential S. H. Ho College of CUHK established in 2006, and the residential colleges of Fudan University launched in 2005, whose characteristics typify residential colleges in China.

As noted in passing, CUHK was founded in 1963 as a federation of three liberal arts colleges. Since 1976, the academic function (department structure and degree programmes) of these three colleges were centralised to the university's faculties of Arts, Science, Business, Engineering and Education. The role of the colleges changed. While the colleges continued to provide accommodations and pastoral care for their students, they were also responsible for providing some general education. In 2012, the undergraduate curriculum in publicly-funded universities in Hong Kong changed from a three-year system to a four-year one. CUHK added five new colleges, thus being able to offer on-campus housing to more than 50% of the undergraduate students. Some of these new colleges became fully residential, requiring their students to reside in college for the entirety of the four years of undergraduate study. One such example is the S. H. Ho College, housing a total of 600 students. In addition to daily and extra-curricular activities, the college offers two three-credit college general education courses, accounting for more than a quarter of the total credit requirement for general education. The purpose of college general education at CUHK across all the colleges is to express the "mission and traditions of each constituent college" and contribute to "the holistic development of students to become responsible citizens of the world". The S. H. Ho College's motto is "Culture, Morals, Devotion, Trustworthiness". Its educational vision is to nurture students with "a refined appreciation of culture, high moral standards, and a strong sense of responsibility and integrity". The two "core founding concepts" of the college centre on imbuing the warmth of "home" and offering distinctive out-of-class learning opportunities. The latter is also known in educational circles as the second classroom.

Fudan University announced to establish Fudan College in 2005 as a teaching, research and administrative institution for the implementation of general education in the university. It was at that time responsible for the education and teaching management of all first-year and part of second-year undergraduate students. Concurrently, drawing on the practices of residential colleges in overseas universities and carrying on the cultural tradition of Chinese *shuyuan*, four colleges were established under Fudan College, namely Zhide College, Tengfei College, Keqing College and Renzhong College, with learning and self-cultivation as the core values, supplemented by transformation and care. The combination of the residential college system and the academic tutor system, complemented by a liberal studies core curriculum, promoted a holistic approach to general education. First-year students lived and studied together in colleges, regardless of their affiliated faculties. Each college was a residential building that not only served as a living space for students, but also as a space for students to exchange academic ideas, discuss life experiences, develop a sense of community, and enhance their consciousness. After the first year of college life at Fudan College, each new student was expected to be able to set far-sighted goals, build a strong academic foundation, refine their characters, cultivate the spirit of Fudan, as well as pave the way for learning in their majors and their all-round

development in the following three years.

In 2012, Fudan University announced that the new Fudan College would be re-organised as an undergraduate college. It was to incorporate Xide College, established the previous year, to form the five residential colleges under the Fudan College umbrella. The college has thus been transformed from an administrative unit to a functional entity. It changed from being responsible for the overall management, learning and cultivation of students in the foundational first year, to assuming responsibility for the all-round development of students as a "second classroom" throughout the undergraduate years. Students are also grouped by majors into specific colleges by certain broadly-defined disciplinary categories; for instances, engineering and technology students were in Tengfei College, humanities and management students in Renzhong College, and science students in Xide College.

Fudan University's stated goals in nurturing talents are: "to foster builders and successors of socialism with an all-around development in morality, intellect, physique, aesthetics and hands-on labour. It stands for an education characterised by 'national identity, humanism, scientific spirit, professionalism, and an international outlook', so as to nurture more talented leaders, professional elite, and cream of society, for the prosperity of the country, the development of society and the advancement of human civilisation. Lastly, it commits to nurture Fudan men and women who will be responsible for national rejuvenation and for making a better future". The residential colleges are serving as a major vehicle to realise the Fudan's education mission.

Residential colleges are recently springing up all over China. The first Education Forum on University Residential College Systems was held at Beihang University in 2014, where a residential college alliance was established. By 2021, seven such fora had been held at different universities, attended by thousands of scholars from over a hundred universities, and five volumes of essays had been published. Overall, publication of research papers written in Chinese on residential colleges proliferated, with topics investigated becoming more in-depth and research quality rising steadily. Although the design of the residential college system and the allocation of resources vary greatly from one university to another, the common thread is the recognition that universities must nurture the character of students in addition to imparting and creating knowledge. In the light of the above, the community

education function of residential colleges is admittedly
one of the most effective mechanisms for nurturing the
character of university students at present.

澳门大学正门
Main entrance of University of Macau

澳大校园内人工湖
Artificial lake of University of Macau

第二部分 | PART 2

试行及实践时期的
澳大住宿式书院

Trial Run and Implementation Phase of
UM Residential College Education

第三章

缘起和理念

2009 年，全国人民代表大会常务委员会批准澳大在中国广东省横琴岛建设新校区，并授权由澳门特别行政区依照澳门特区法律实施管辖。同年 12 月 20 日，国家主席胡锦涛亲临新校区主持奠基仪式。中央政府和特区政府自此赋予澳大一个更重大的历史使命：建设世界一流的大学。2013 年，国务院副总理汪洋主持新校区启用仪式。2014 年，顺利完成迁校，正式在新校区上课。同年 12 月 20 日国家主席习近平视察了澳大新校区，赞扬澳大在办学制度理念上有很多的创新。澳大有了新校区，更有机会大力发展本科教育。

现今大学不能仅仅满足于完善学术教育，因为在这瞬息万变的社会中，很多学术知识都不能保鲜，往往在学生毕业前，一些所学知识已经过时、落后。因此，大学的任务非仅限于学术教育，亦须担负起为学生提供一系列不同类型的体验式学习经历，以激发学生个人发展的动力和社会责任感的工作。在这种教育理念下，学术教育依然为大学之基本任务，但不能像研究型高等教育那样只重视学术教育。为更能适应这个不断变化的新时代及为社会做出贡献，学生需要走出课堂以发展多元化技能，培养创造力、原创思维、逻辑推理能力、伦理感、灵活应变能力及乐观态度。要培养这些实用技能及态度，书院的社群教育是一种行之有效的方法，主要是因为在书院里，学习并不仅限于课堂中，更多是在课堂外和同辈之间的互动及影响中。这种通过社群学习的高等教育模式，在世界很多一流大学累积了大量的实践经验，卓有成效。鉴于此，澳大在构建新校区时，锐意革新，由走读型大学改为一所住宿型大学，提供传统学科教育以外的社群教育、体验式教育。

首先，澳大确立了本科生教育"才德兼备"的大方向，推行融合专业、通识、研习和社群教育等"四位一体"的教育模式，目的是培养能自我反思、热心助人、有社会责任感，以及能在多元文化和充满挑战性的环境下成长而又学有所成的学生。这是澳大对学生整体性的教育要求，每一位本科生必须达到四个方位的教育要求，方可毕业。

澳大在 2010 年初参考世界一流大学的成功经验，成立了两间试点式书院——东亚书院及珍禧书院，目的是透过这种机制来落实全人教育的理念、"四位一体"的教育模式及以"仁、义、礼、知、信"五常伦理为本的校训。2013 年秋，郑裕彤书院和满珍纪念书院的一年级新生入住新校区南九楼，是新校区首批住校学生。至 2014 年春，各书院陆续完成命名。同年秋，大学新校区正式启用，书院制全面推行。当时共八间书院，除更名后的何鸿燊东亚书院和霍英东珍禧书院外，并有郑裕彤书院、满珍纪念书院、绍邦书院、蔡继有书院、吕志和书院及曹光彪书院。2014 年，习近平主席视察澳大时，莅访郑裕彤书院，鼓励师生传承和发扬中国传统文化。2016 年，马万祺罗柏心书院及张昆仑书院成立，澳大十间书院的格局遂告完成，共可容纳 5000 多名住宿生。书院社群教育，也成为澳大本科生教育不可或缺的一环。所有一年级本科生，均随机分派到各书院。每间书院学生的主修专业，原则上尽量维持多元化。所有本科生都同时拥有双重身份，既属于主修专业所属学院，又属于一间书院。

书院是新校区的亮点，占整个校园面积近五分之一。它可以在课堂以外培养学生的软实力，是大学教育的重要组成部分。在这个大胆探索、勇敢尝试的新时代，书院系统的建立是澳大历史上浓墨重

澳门大学图书馆正门
Main entrance of University of Macau Library

彩的一笔，使澳大成为一所真正意义上的书院式大学，为人才培养明确了方向并提供了有效模式。书院系统也标志着澳大实现了从传统院系结构大学到书院式大学的巨大转变，确立了澳大在当代社会的地位，为学生成长创造了良好的条件，也增强了家长对澳大教育的信心，并为毕业生在社会上赢得更多的尊重。澳大提供的教育不仅具有潜在的价值，而且在澳门甚至更大的范围内产生了可观的社会影响。

澳大全面推行的书院系统，给予了本科生更多的成长辅导及多方位的教育，与学院专业教育与通识教育相辅相成。书院学习乃为"育人"，学生以体验式、全方位、全天候的方式，学习专业课程外的软实力。书院采取课程化的规划方式，使本科生获得体验式经历，并通过制定能力指标和评鉴制度以确保学生在毕业时能够达到社群教育的要求。书院作为澳大社群教育重要的一环，其核心的教育目的，就是通过系统化学习规划，利用所有课程、项目计划、校内外活动等体验式学习方法，培养学生各方面的兴趣，增强他们的能力，以达到书院教育的五项能力指标，包括具有国际视野的公民、人际关系与团队合作、领导与服务、文化参与以及健康生活。

书院社群教育对学生的学习要求包括三个层面：一是达到一般书院教育要求；二是达到个别书院教育的特别要求；三是达到学生个人自我发展的要求。为了评估学生是否达到社群教育的要求，书院制定了三个评鉴学生的方法，包括自我评鉴、同侪评鉴、老师评鉴。所有评鉴都是形成式而非竞争式，会在学生进入书院学习的四年内持续进行。由于每名学生皆不同，书院不使用单一标准去对他们进行评估，因此学生学习成效评估不具有竞争性，

书院举办中国茶文化体验活动
Experiencing Chinese tea culture in the RC

而是基于学生自身的发展。

　　此外，如评估书院的软实力一般使用定性研究，很少使用定量研究。成效评估的目的是单独分析每个学生在校期间有没有进步。因此，用于记录每名学生所参与的活动和感想的学生电子档案平台，成了重要的自我评估工具。另外，大学会定期进行问卷调查，追踪学生的成长。书院教学人员亦经常与学生交流，观察他们的成长。以个人评语或小组讨论方式进行的同侪评鉴也能够达到评估的目的。

书院中庭景致
The courtyard of a RC

Chapter 3

Origin and Philosophy

In 2009, the Standing Committee of the National People's Congress approved the construction of a new campus for UM on Hengqin Island in Guangdong Province of China, and authorised the Macao SAR to exercise jurisdiction over the new campus in accordance with the laws of the SAR. On 20th December in the same year, Hu Jintao, President of the People's Republic of China, personally presided over the ground-breaking ceremony for the new campus. Since then, the central government and the Macao SAR government entrusted the UM with an important historic mission: to become a world-class university. In 2013, Wang Yang, Vice Premier of the State Council, presided over the inauguration of the new campus. In 2014, campus relocation was successfully completed and classes officially commenced in the new campus. In the same year, President Xi Jinping made an inspection of the new campus on 20th December and offered his endorsement of UM's many innovative ideas in higher education. The new campus has provided UM with the conditions and opportunity to strengthen and further develop its undergraduate education.

Higher education institutions today cannot simply focus on providing academic education only. In this rapidly changing society, academic knowledge may swiftly become outdated. More often than not, even before they graduate, some of the knowledge that have learnt may become outdated and lag behind current advances. Given this situation, the mission of universities cannot be limited to academic education, but should instead include the goal of providing students with a series of different experiential learning experiences intended to stimulate their personal development and instil a sense of social responsibility. With this broader educational concept, while academic education remains a basic

responsibility of universities, it cannot be their primary focus in educating students as for the research-oriented institutions. To better adapt to this new era of constant change and contribute to society, students need to go outside their classrooms in order to develop diverse skills, creativity, original thinking, analytical reasoning, ethics, adaptability and optimism. The community education in RCs is an effective means to cultivate these practical skills and attitudes, mainly because learning in the RCs extends beyond the classroom and involves interaction with and influence of peers in different settings. Such a community learning model for higher education has been in practice at many leading universities in the world, with proven success. This model has also proven to be highly successful. In light of this, when constructing the new campus, the UM decided to transform itself from a university primarily for commuter students into a collegiate university, offering community and experiential education through RCs in complementary to traditional discipline-specific education.

At the outset, the university set the twin goals of fostering both talent and virtue as the general direction for its undergraduate education by adopting the unique and pioneering 4-in-1 education model consisting of discipline-specific education, general education, research and internship education, and community and peer education. The aim here is to nurture self-reflective, caring and socially responsible students who will be able to grow and achieve in a multicultural and challenging environment. This educational model embodies the university's overall educational vision for our students, and each undergraduate student must fulfil requirements in all four aspects in order to graduate.

In early 2010, by referencing the successful

澳门大学校园内的连廊设计贯通整个校园
The corridor design of University of Macau connects the entire campus.

澳门大学住宿式书院建筑外观
Architectural feature of the RC of University of Macau

学生可以在书院里认识不同专业、不同年级的学生
Students can make friends with peers from different majors and years in the RC.

experiences of top universities around the world, UM established two pilot RCs, namely the East Asia College and the Pearl Jubilee College with the intention that RCs would be the main instrument of implementing whole-person education, as embodied by the 4-in-1 education model as well as the five virtues listed in the university motto: humanity, integrity, propriety, wisdom, and sincerity. In the fall of 2013, first-year students of Cheng Yu Tung College （CYTC） and Moon Chun Memorial College （MCMC） moved into the S9 building, becoming the first cohort to live in the new campus. Other RCs were successively named and established through the following spring. In the fall of 2014, the new campus was officially inaugurated with the RC system fully up and running. At that time, there were a total of eight RCs, including CYTC, MCMC, Shiu Pong College （SPC）, Choi Kai Yau College （CKYC）, Lui Che Woo College （LCWC）, Chao Kuang Piu College （CKPC）, in addition to the original two pilot colleges that were renamed Stanley Ho East Asia College （SEAC） and Henry Fok Pearl Jubilee College （FPJC）. In the same year, President Xi Jinping visited the CYTC during his visit to UM. He encouraged teachers and students to treasure, enrich, and promote the heritage of traditional Chinese culture. With the openings of Ma Man Kei and Lo Pak Sam College （MLC） and Cheong Kun Lun College （CKLC） in 2016, the university finally completed the construction project on all 10 RCs, which together can accommodate more than 5,000 students. The community education provided in the RCs has also become an integral part of UM's undergraduate education. All first-year undergraduate students are randomly assigned to the RCs, applying the principle that the student who bodies at each RC has as much

diversity as possible in terms of students' subject areas. Thus, all undergraduate students are required to have a dual identity; that is, each of them belongs to the faculty of their major subject and to a RC.

The RCs are the highlight of the new campus, occupying nearly one-fifth of the entire campus area. They are an important part of the university's educational framework as they serve to cultivate students' soft skills outside the classroom. In this era of bold exploration and experimentation, the establishment of the RC system represents a momentous episode in UM's history. It makes UM a truly collegiate university, and offers a clear direction and model for talent cultivation. It also represents UM's massive transformation from a traditional faculty-based institution to a collegiate university. This consolidates UM's position in contemporary society and creates favourable ambience and an enriching environment for students' development and growth. Moreover, the system also strengthens parents' confidence in UM's education and earns UM graduates greater respect in the community. The education provided by UM not only has the potential of transformative effect on the students, but also makes a considerable social impact in Macao and beyond.

UM's full implementation of the RC system provides undergraduate students with more mentoring and a well-rounded education, which complement the discipline-specific and general education offered by the faculties. Learning in the RCs is about character building, in that the RCs enable students to acquire soft skills, which are not covered in academic subjects, in an experiential, multifaceted

高桌晚宴、院长晚宴邀请校内外嘉宾主讲的专题讲座，深受学生欢迎
High table dinners and master dinners with guest speakers to give lectures are well received by students.

and continual way. The RC education adopts a curriculum-based approach in its programmes to provide experiential learning for undergraduate students with a set of competencies and an assessment system to ensure that students meet the requirements of community education by graduation. As an essential part of UM's community education, the RCs have the core educational purpose of spurring students' interests and enhancing their abilities in various areas through systematically planned learning opportunities via courses, projects, and other experiential learning activities on and off campus. The five target competencies of RC education are, namely, citizenship with a global perspective, interpersonal relationships and teamwork, leadership and service, cultural engagement, and healthy lifestyle.

The learning requirements of the RC community education consist of three dimensions. The first is to achieve the general requirements of RC education; the second is to meet the special requirements specific to each RC; and the third is to attain the goals for students' personal development. To assess whether or not students have achieved a satisfactory level of the community education, the RCs have developed three types of assessments, namely, self-assessment, peer assessment and teacher assessment. All these assessments are formative rather than competitive, and assessment is continual throughout the four years of the student's affiliation with a RC. Considering the uniqueness of each student, the RCs do not use a single yardstick and assessments of students' learning outcomes are not based on competition, but rather on the students' own development.

In addition, soft skills such as the five competencies in the RC education are generally assessed qualitatively, and quantitative methods are rarely used. As outcome assessments aim to individually analyse each student's improvement over their university years, the student e-portfolio platform, which is used to record the activities each student joins and their reflections, has become an important self-assessment tool. The university also conducts regular questionnaire surveys to track the development of students. RCs' academic staff, too, interact with the students regularly to observe their progress. Peer reviews in the forms of individual comments or group discussion also serve the purpose of evaluation.

第四章

组织及教育活动

　　澳大书院有统一的人员配制，每个书院都有全职驻院教学人员，包括院长、副院长及两名导师。院长由具有卓越学术研究成果、丰富教学与行政经验，以及在专业领域有广泛国际关系网络的教授出任，引领书院的总体发展。副院长监督书院日常运作、学生事务及书院秩序。两名导师则协助院长及副院长为近 500 名学生安排不同类型的活动。教学人员为书院社群的一员，与学生们同宿共膳，通过参与学生们的日常生活，认识每位学生，并引导学生互相影响及学习。书院经常举办各类大小型活动，部分由教学人员筹办，其他的在教学人员指导下由学生主办或协办，从而提供不同的机会和平台以开阔学生的视野及丰富经验，致力发展他们的领导能力和沟通技巧，灌输服务社会的理念。教学人员也定期跟进学生的专业学习进度，给予学生适当的学术支持及鼓励。此外，书院亦有三名全职行政人员，专门负责书院财务、行政工作，楼宇维修及优化工程，并为教学人员及学生举办活动提供支持。

　　除上述全职驻院教学人员之外，各书院另有数十名以上来自各专业学院的非驻院教学人员。事实上，澳大规定全职教学人员，除授课及科研外，也需为学生的课外活动等非常规教育提供支持。他们经常出席书院活动，为学生提供专业学术指导，或在他们自己所擅长的领域对学生进行辅导，如辩论、烹饪、绘画、茶道、运动、音乐等。

　　书院设立各种类型的学生组织及岗位以协助管理整个书院社群，当中包括由全体院生自行选出骨干成员的院生会，院生会下设多个不同的工作组，为学生提供各类活动。书院在每楼层都派驻书院助教（由研究生担任）或书院助理（由高年级本科生担任）作楼层助理，他们协助照顾住宿生的日常生活。为推动书院系统中的集体活动（如运动竞赛、大型演讲等），各书院学生代表组成跨书院委员会，并由书院导师给予指导。

　　书院鼓励学生组织及其成员，举办各种各样的活动，以实现书院的使命和响应学生的需求。这些活动包括高桌晚宴、院长晚宴、由校内外嘉宾主讲的专题讲座或座谈会、兴趣小组、工作坊、楼层活动、书院间的竞赛及与其他院校的交流活动等。活动项目涉及社交、艺术、文化、体育、社区服务、英语学习、学生领导力培养等。此外，中英文辩论、体育竞赛、啦啦队比赛、歌舞表演等，也使书院生活更有活力、更加精彩。

团队协作是书院教育其中的一个胜任力，培养学生的人际关系及团队精神
Teamwork is one of the competencies in RC education, which cultivates students' interpersonal relationships and team spirit.

书院致力于营造浓厚的学习氛围，鼓励学生在课余时间进行学术讨论
RCs are committed to creating an academic learning ambience and encouraging students to facilitate academic exchange after class.

Chapter 4

Organisation and Educational Activities

All RCs in UM have a standardised staffing organisation. Full-time resident academic staff include the college master, the associate master and two resident fellows. The college master directs the overall development of the RC. They are normally accomplished professors with excellent academic and research achievements, who possess rich teaching and administrative experience and maintain an extensive international network in their fields of expertise. The associate master oversees the day-to-day operation of the college, student affairs and discipline in the college. The two resident fellows assist the college master and the associate master in organising different kinds of activities for around 500 students. As members of the college community, the resident academic staff share the same living environment with the students. Through involving themselves in students' daily lives, they get to know each of them and guide them to influence and learn from each other. The RCs frequently host a wide variety of activities. Some are organised by the academic staff, while others are organised or co-organised by the students under the guidance of the former. This provides opportunities and various platforms for students to broaden their horizons and experiences, develop leadership and communication skills and foster a sense of community service. Additionally, the academic staff regularly follow up on the students' academic progress and provide appropriate academic support and encouragement. There are also three full-time administrative staff in each college, who are responsible for the college's finance, administration and co-ordination of building maintenance and improvement, as well as providing support for the academic staff and students in organising activities.

In addition to the full-time resident academic staff mentioned above, each RC has dozens of affiliated non-resident academic staff from all faculties. In fact, the university requires all full-time academic staff to provide support in students' extra-curricular activities outside the conventional classroom setting, along with their teaching and research duties. They regularly attend RC events, offering academic guidance to students, and/ or hosting extra-curricular activities that they themselves are good at, such as debating, cooking, drawing, performing tea ceremonies, sports and music.

Each RC has established various student bodies and positions to assist in managing the RC community. There is the House Association (HA). With key executive members elected by the whole RC student population, the working groups of the HA organise many activities for students. There are also resident tutors (who are graduate students) and resident assistants (who are senior undergraduate students) on each floor, who help take care of the daily needs of the students on their respective floors. Moreover, an inter-college committee is formed by student representatives from each college, which under the guidance of resident fellows, organises joint events involving all the RCs, for example, sporting competitions and large-scale public speeches.

The RC encourages student organisations and their members to promote a wide range of activities in order to realise the mission of the RC and respond to students' needs. These activities include high-table dinners, master's dinners, lectures and seminars by internal or external guest speakers, interest groups, workshops, floor activities, inter-college competitions and exchange activities with other institutions. These events cover aspects of social life, arts and culture, sports, community service, English learning, student leadership training, etc. There are also Chinese- and English-speaking debating tournaments, sporting events, cheerleading contests, singing and dance performances, which add to the vibrancy and excitement of RC life.

何鸿燊东亚书院 / 工商管理学院 / 李芷倩
Stanley Ho East Asia College / Faculty of Business Administration / Lei Chi Sin
2021—2022 学年 书院院生会副主席
Academic Year 2021—2022 Vice President of House Association

"我们一起携手解决疑难，冲破难关，种种经历令我们更团结，感觉书院就是我们第二个家。"

"Residential college is a second home where we are united to solve problems, overcome difficulties and share our feelings."

吕志和书院 / 科技学院 / 林霖
Lui Che Woo College / Faculty of Science and Technology / Lam Lam
2021—2022 学年 书院第五届书院大使
Academic Year 2021—2022 The 5th Batch of College Ambassador

"书院大使工作加强了我对澳大以及书院的归属感，希望未来有更多同学可以在书院生活中一起探索自己的另一面。"

"Taking up the duty of an ambassador has enhanced my sense of belonging to the University and to the residential college. I hope more students can kick off their self-discovery journey in their residential college life."

蔡继有书院 / 工商管理学院 / 马竞坤
Choi Kai Yau College / Faculty of Business Administration / Ma Jingkun
2021—2022 学年 书院院生会秘书长
Academic Year 2021—2022 Secretary-General of House Association

"我连续两年参加书院的啦啦队，从中我不仅掌握了啦啦队的动作技巧，更重要的是，我学到了团队精神的重要性。"

"I have participated in the cheerleading team of the residential college for two consecutive years, from which I not only mastered the cheerleading skills, but more importantly, I learned the importance of team spirit."

绍邦书院 / 工商管理学院 / 朱俊恒
Shiu Pong College / Faculty of Business Administration / Chu Chon Hang
2021—2022 学年 书院院生会副主席
Academic Year 2021—2022 Vice President of House Association

"这学年最让我难忘的活动莫过于中秋游园会了，虽然筹备过程中遇到不少困难和问题，但幸好最后在大家的共同努力下还是圆满举行了。"

"The most memorable activity of this academic year was the Mid-Autumn Festival Party. Although there were many problems to tackle in the process, I am pleased that it was successfully completed in the end."

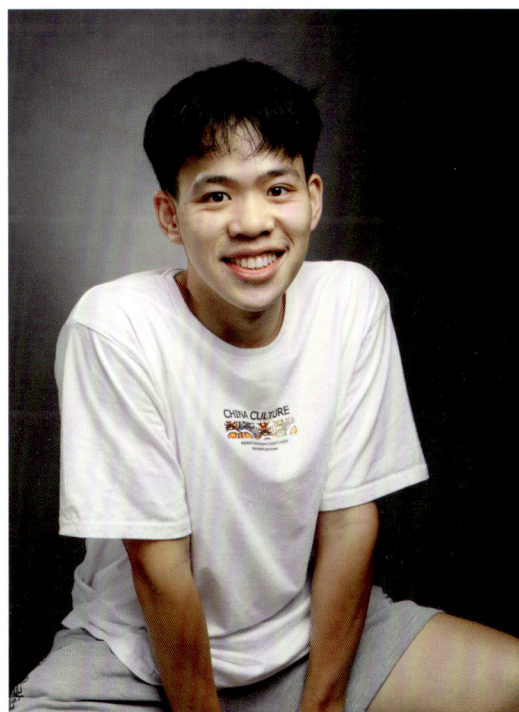

蔡继有书院 / 科技学院 / 欧阳铭聪
Choi Kai Yau College / Faculty of Science and Technology / Ouyang Mingcong
2018—2019 学年 毕业生
Academic Year 2018—2019 Graduate

"通过书院我看到了学生生活精彩的一面，只要愿意用心投入，就会发现书院生活可以比想象中更精彩，是一辈子的回忆，值得回味的青春。"

"I have seen another wonderful side of student life in residential college. As long as I am willing to devote myself, residential college life can be much more exciting and enjoyable than ever imagined. Those precious memories of my youth will last for a lifetime."

何鸿燊东亚书院 / 人文学院 /
Hannah Keely Sin
Stanley Ho East Asia College / Faculty of Arts and Humanities / Hannah Keely Sin
2021—2022 学年 书院学生助理
Academic Year 2021—2022 Resident Assistant

"书院生活让我们有机会探索新事物，以不同的方式提升自己。"

"Residential college life gives us opportunities to explore something new, enhance ourselves in different ways."

张昆仑书院 / 教育学院 / 梁敏芝
Cheong Kun Lun College / Faculty of Education / Leong Man Chi
2020—2021 学年 书院学生助理
Academic Year 2021—2022 Resident Assistant

"在三年书院生活中，我认识了很好的朋友，参与书院服务的经历也让我学习到很多为人处世的方法。对我来说，住在书院不只是为了满足学校要求，它更是一种宝贵的经历。"

"The three-year residential college experience has earned me good friends and excellent interpersonal skills. For me, living in RC is more of a valuable experience than just a university requirement."

郑裕彤书院 / 人文学院 / 林霞远
Cheng Yu Tung College / Faculty of Arts and Humanities / Lin Xiayuan
2020—2021 学年 书院学生助理
Academic Year 2021—2022 Resident Assistant

"书院不仅锻炼了我组织活动、与人沟通的能力，还鼓励我积极参与服务学习项目，做个有社会担当的大学生。"

"I learned how to become an activity organiser and a good communicator in residential college. RC also encourages me to actively engage in service learning programmes and be a responsible university student."

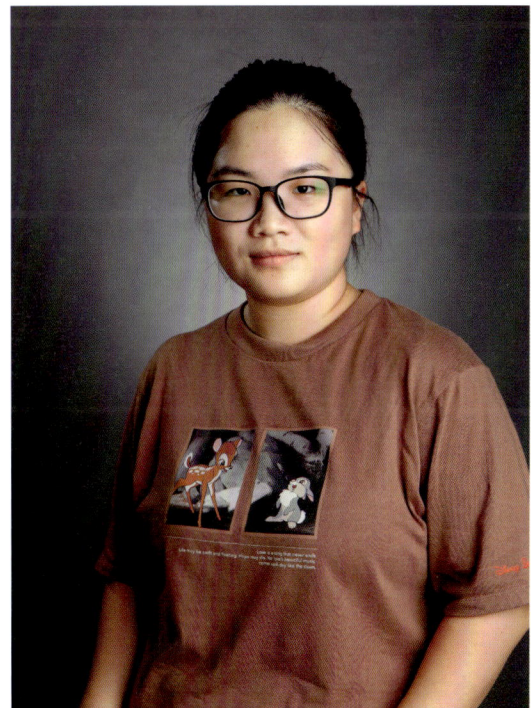

曹光彪书院 / 人文学院 / 欧淑祯
**Chao Kuang Piu College / Faculty of Arts
and Humanities / Ao Sok Cheng**
2021—2022 学年 书院学生助理
Academic Year 2021—2022 Resident Assistant

"书院代表的就是家，在院长、导师及办公室行政人员的陪伴下，来自不同地方、不同学系的我们一起生活成长，共同分享生活中的喜怒哀乐。与此同时，它更是一个探索自我、发挥所长的舞台，谢谢书院，谢谢在这段旅程中遇见的每一位。"

"Residential college is like a second home. Accompanied by the college master, resident fellows and administrative staff, here we share our growth and every bit of our life together, despite differences in cultural and disciplinary background. Meanwhile it is also a platform for self-discovery and achievement. Thank you RC and everyone I met in this fruitful journey."

张昆仑书院 / 科技学院 / 黄子健
**Cheong Kun Lun College / Faculty of Science
and Technology / Wong Chi Kin**
2021—2022 学年 书院学生助理
Academic Year 2021—2022 Resident Assistant

"我参与和协助举办多元化的书院活动，在助人为乐、关怀院生的同时，也充实了自我，丰富了大家的学生生活。"

"I have achieved self-improvement and enriched the student life of myself and everyone, through participation and organisation of residential college activities."

霍英东珍禧书院 / 社会科学学院 / 黄茵
Henry Fok Pearl Jubilee College / Faculty of Social Sciences / Huang Yin
2016—2017 学年 毕业生
Academic Year 2016—2017 Graduate

"书院让我看到了团结的力量，我学会了如何统筹活动、如何与他人沟通合作。我在书院不但结识了很好的朋友，更找到了现在创业团队的合伙人。感谢书院，感恩经历。"

"I learned how to coordinate activities and cooperate with people, and more importantly, the power of unity in my RC life. I have made very good friends of my life, as well as the partners of my current entrepreneurial team. I am grateful for my residential college experience."

马万祺罗柏心书院 / 工商管理学院 / 刘丰瑞
Ma Man Kei And Lo Pak Sam College / Faculty of Business Administration / Liu Fengrui
2021—2022 学年 书院学生助理
Academic Year 2021—2022 Resident Assistant

"在大三上学期的夏天我作为学生助理，协助新同学办理入住手续、参加以及举办活动的经历，至今还让我记忆犹新。"

"When I was a third-year student, I was a residential assistant who assisted new students to move in. The experiences of participating and organising activities have been unforgettable."

张昆仑书院 / 人文学院 / 何淑莹
Cheong Kun Lun College / Faculty of Arts and Humanities / Ho Sok Ieng
2020—2021 学年 书院学生助理
Academic Year 2020—2021 Resident Assistant

"书院让我有更多的学习时间，给予我良好的学习氛围和各种各样提升自我的机会。我也在书院认识了一群好朋友，在此留下了很多美好的回忆。"

"I managed to spend more time to study in residential college. This favourable environment offers me with lots of learning opportunities and good memories. Here in RC, I met my first new friends in residential college when I first arrived at UM."

马万祺罗柏心书院 / 教育学院 / 刘慧仪
Ma Man Kei And Lo Pak Sam College / Faculty of Education / Lao Wai I
2020—2021 学年 English Salon 主席
2021—2022 学年 书院院生会秘书长
Academic Year 2020—2021 President of English Salon
Academic Year 2021—2022 Secretary-General of House Association

"在组织书院活动的过程中，我学会了如何与他人合作，换位思考，提升自己的策划能力和建立互相包容的团队精神。"

"In the process of organising college activities, I learned how to collaborate with others and stand in other's shoes, while strengthening my planning capabilities and team spirit."

绍邦书院 / 人文学院 / 刘荣钊
Shiu Pong College / Faculty of Arts and Humanities / Lao Weng Chio
2020—2021 学年 书院助教
Academic Year 2020—2021 Resident Tutor

"我曾经是个社交恐惧者，参加书院活动，让我遇到了很多友善优秀的同学、导师、教授，他们的出现告诉我世界无垠，莫作笼中鸟，让我学会放下往事伤痕。"

"I used to have social anxiety. Participating in college activities has allowed me to exchange ideas with different schoolmates, mentors, and professors. I learned from them that the world is boundless. I am thankful for having met with you all."

霍英东珍禧书院 / 人文学院 / 陈飞
Henry Fok Pearl Jubilee College / Faculty of Arts and Humanities / Chen Fei
2021—2022 学年 书院助教
Academic Year 2021—2022 Resident Tutor

"在书院我收获了很多文创及出版的机会，带领不同专业的同学合作出版了六本书，参与了从创作、排版到与出版商及印刷厂合作沟通等环节，对我将来的工作大有帮助。"

"I have gained many opportunities for cultural creativity and publishing during my residential college life. I have co-published six books with students from different academic backgrounds. From creative design skills to pragmatic liaison with publishers and printing houses, the skills I learned are of tremendous help to my career development."

满珍纪念书院 / 社会科学学院 / 梁善衡
Moon Chun Memorial College / Faculty of Social Sciences / Leong Sin Hang

2021—2022 学年 书院院生会秘书长
Academic Year 2021—2022 Secretary-General of House Association

"书院独特的中西文化融合氛围，让我们有幸邀请各国驻澳领事到校交流分享，参与澳门商会举办的活动。拓宽视野的同时，也让我看见自己更多的可能性。"

"The unique international atmosphere of the college encourages us to conduct exchanges with consuls from different countries and to participate in the activities organised by the Macao Chamber of Commerce. While broadening my horizons, it also allows me to discover different sides of myself."

吕志和书院 / 科技学院 / 王晓明
Lui Che Woo College / Faculty of Science and Technology / Wang Xiaoming

2021—2022 学年 书院助教
Academic Year 2021—2022 Resident Tutor

"我在书院举办过运动类、艺术体验等活动。书院便是院生的生活圈和朋友圈，而书院的老师则像家长一般关心和照顾院生。书院是一个大家庭，亦是一个大学的缩影。"

"I have conducted various kinds of activities in residential college. It is a big family and a community where students live and socialise with their friends, and where academic staff provide pastoral care for students."

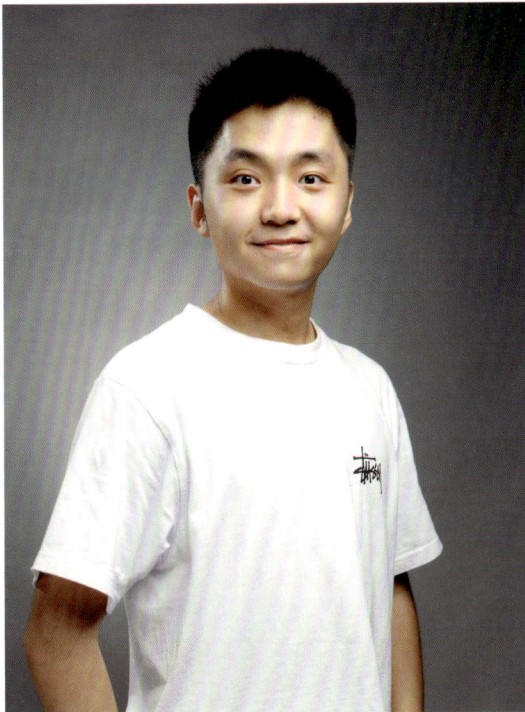

郑裕彤书院 / 工商管理学院 / 荣誉学院 / 侯振炜
Cheng Yu Tung College / Faculty of Business Administration / Honours College / Hao Chan Wai
2021—2022 学年 书院学生助理
Academic Year 2021—2022 Resident Assistant

"我曾经是院生会的体育健康组组员、院生会主席、书院篮球队主力，现在是学生助理、创新创业团队的一员，其中的身份转变让我学会感同身受，换个角度看待世界，收获良多。"

"I have played several different roles such as the member of Sports and Health Working Group, the President of the House Association and the key player of the college basketball team. I am currently a resident assistant and a member of the innovation and entrepreneurship team. I gained a lot from those identities and responsibilities, such as empathy and critical thinking."

满珍纪念书院 / 社会科学学院 / 林家仪
Moon Chun Memorial College / Faculty of Social Sciences / Lam Ka I
2021—2022 学年 书院院生会主席
Academic Year 2021—2022 President of House Association

"感谢书院提供了一个很好的平台让我发掘自己的才能。每一件在学院与书院学习到的事情，不论大小，都成为我创业起步的基础。"

"Thanks to residential college for providing me with a good platform to explore my talents. Everything I learned here, no matter how big or small, has become the foundation for my entrepreneurship."

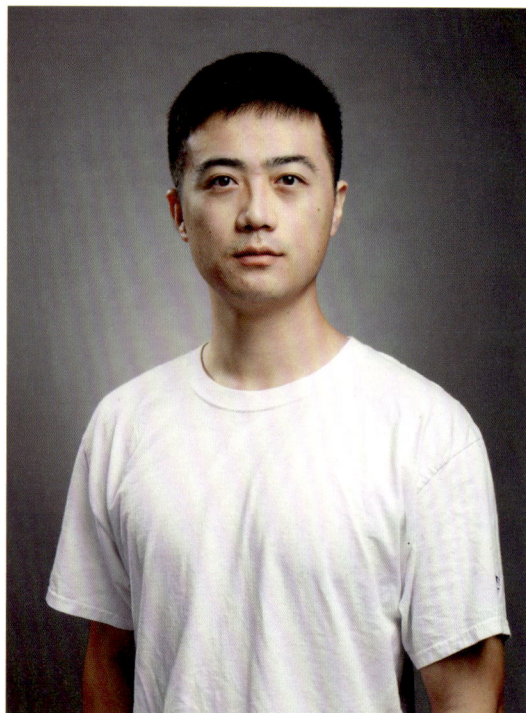

曹光彪书院 / 科技学院 / 丁子钦
Chao Kuang Piu College / Faculty of Science and Technology / Ding Ziqin
2021—2022 学年 无限咖啡创办人
Academic Year 2021—2022 Founder of INFINITECOFFEE

"有机会做自己喜欢的事情并分享给他人是一种幸运，抱着这样的心态，我和一群志同道合的朋友在书院创办了 INFINITECOFFEE。感谢这个机遇让我学会如何分配任务，提升团队的工作效率，共同进步。"

"It was lucky for me to do my favorite thing and share it with others. My like-mind friends and I set up INFINITECOFFEE in residential college holding such a mindset. Thanks to this, I have the opportunity to advance myself, to assign tasks, improve teamwork efficiency and make progress together."

张超彦 / Cheong Chio In
东亚书院第一届院生会主席
1st President of House Association of East Asia College

"院生会的体验让我往后一直积极参与及从事一些提高青年领导力和创造力的工作，我现在是浙江省青联委员和粤港澳大湾区青年总会副主任，同时亦是澳门多间企业的负责人。"

"My experience in House Association paved the way for my engagement in youth leadership and creative work in the years that followed. I am currently a member of the Zhejiang Youth Federation and the Deputy Director of the Guangdong-Hong Kong-Macao Greater Bay Area Youth Federation. I am also the person in charge of many companies in Macao."

郑裕彤书院创业团队
Start-up Project Team of Cheng Yu Tung College
廖俊辉 / 郭芷晴 / 谭凯盈
Lio Chon Fai / Kwok Tsz Ching / Tam Hoi Ieng
郑裕彤书院导师 邓宇明
健康科学学院副教授 谭建业
Dr. Tang Yu Ming, Resident Fellow, Cheng Yu Tung College; Prof. Tam Kin Yip, Associate Professor, Faculty of Health Science

"尽管书院不是创孵中心，但也为我们提供了全面的帮助，我们共同面对失败，也共同分享成功的喜悦，感谢书院对我们团队的支持。"

"Although RC is not an incubation center, its support to us is crucial and comprehensive. We face failures and share the joy of success together. We are thankful for having the support from our residential college."

第五章 / Chapter 5

图说住宿式书院设施
Snapshots of Facilities in Residential Colleges

住宿式书院内均建有庭院以便举办各种活动
RCs are equipped with courtyards for hosting various activities

书院中庭、书院岛一区以及周边景致
RC quad, RC Island One, and perimeter landscape

图书馆、卧房、研习室、静思室、洗衣房
Library, bedroom, study room, contemplation room, laundry room

茶水间、食堂、课室
Pantry, dinning hall, classroom

小讲堂、书院会议及会客室
Small lecture hall, conference and reception room

健身房、音乐室、摄影棚、咖啡座、厨艺室、休息室
Gym, music room, photography studio, cafe, cooking classroom, lounge

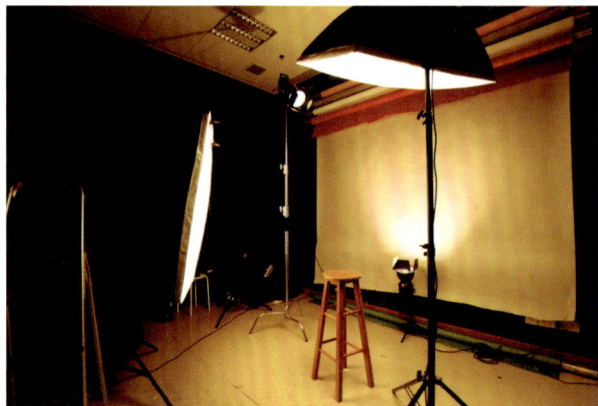

第六章 / Chapter 6

图说住宿式书院试行及实践时期的五大能力指标教育

Pictures Illustrating the Training of the Five Competencies during the Trial Run and Implementation Phase

1.

具国际视野的公民
Citizenship with global perspectives

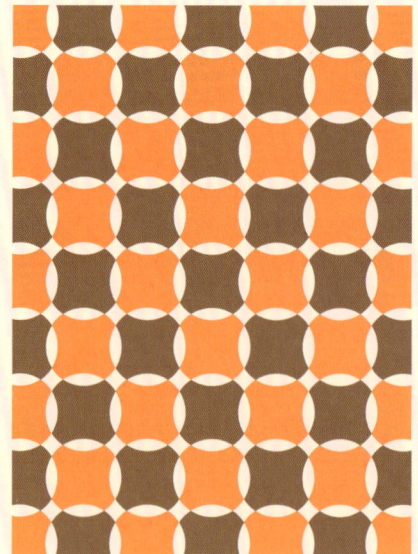

绍邦书院 提升英语·开拓视野系列
SPC's English language enhancement and
eye-opening series

蔡继有书院 南京历史文化交流系列
CKYC's cultural and historical exchange series

吕志和书院 认识澳门，了解国情系列
LCWC's knowing Macao and national education series

马万祺罗柏心书院 境内外服务系列
MLC's service series in the mainland and overseas

马万祺罗柏心书院 多语多元文化项目
MLC's multilingual and multicultural programmes

张昆仑书院 粤港澳大湾区学习考察系列
CKLC's Greater Bay Area study trip series

满珍纪念书院 国际商务活动系列
MCMC's international business series

何鸿燊东亚书院 公民意识教育系列
SEAC's civic awareness education series

郑裕彤书院 马六甲葡萄牙村服务学习计划
CYTC's service learning trips to Melaka
Portuguese settlement
(a Belt and Road Initiative programme)

满珍纪念书院 欧盟系列讲座
MCMC's European Union lecture series

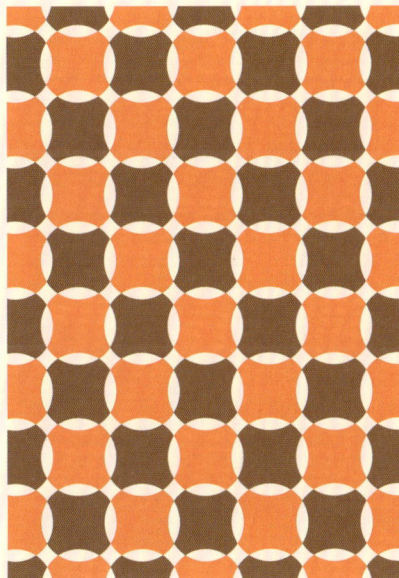

何鸿燊东亚书院 参访澳门监狱项目
SEAC's visit to Macao prison

2.

人际关系与
团队合作

Interpersonal relation
and teamwork

绍邦书院 辩论沟通·逻辑思维项目
SPC's debating and logical thinking programme

郑裕彤书院 学生创业品牌项目
CYTC's student entrepreneurship and branding programme

绍邦书院 公关大使·陶冶品质项目
SPC's student ambassador and qualities
cultivation programme

马万祺罗柏心书院 多维度·跨学科的学术氛围项目
MLC's multi-dimensional inter-disciplinary academic programme

曹光彪书院 学长共习项目
CKPC's alumni mentorship programme

蔡继有书院 同心协作创意项目
CKYC's collaboration in creativity programme

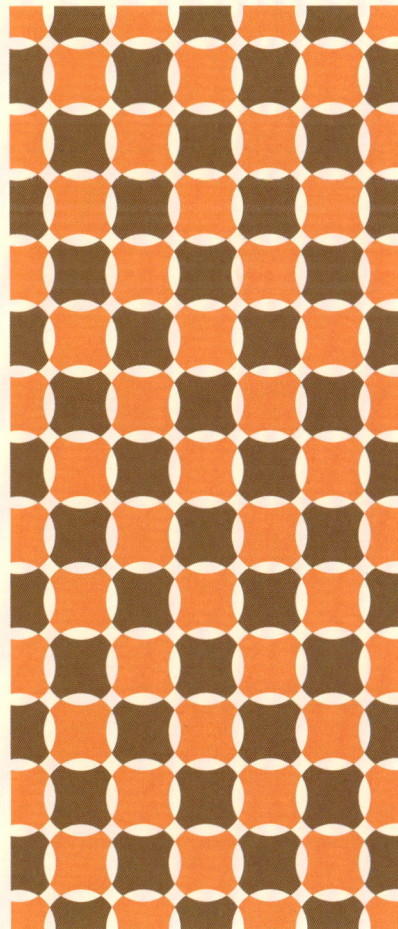

3.

领导与服务
Leadership and service

霍英东珍禧书院 珍禧贵州服务学习项目
FPJC's service learning programme in Guizhou

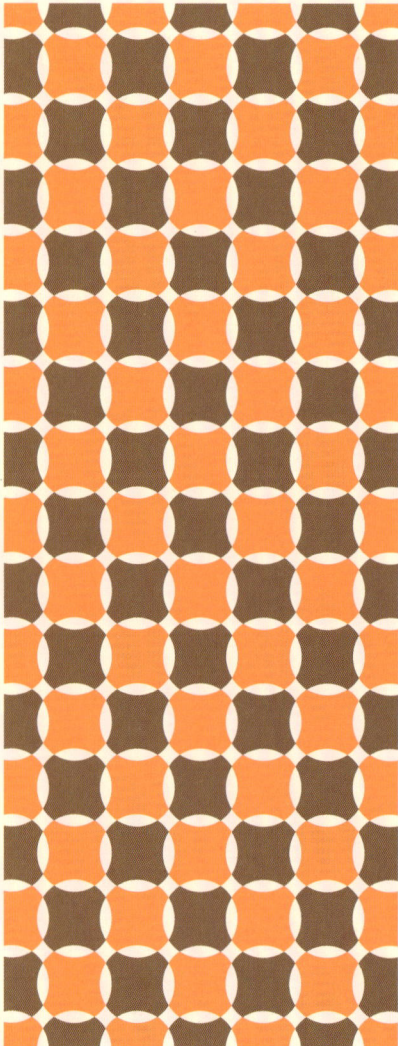

绍邦书院 服务学习·爱无止息项目
SPC's service learning programme

吕志和书院 台风灾后小区支持项目
LCWC's post-typhoon support programme

曹光彪书院 义教团
CKPC's voluntary teaching team

马万祺罗柏心书院 义工制度项目
MLC's volunteering mechanism project

张昆仑书院 湖北服务学习计划
CKLC's service learning programme in Hubei

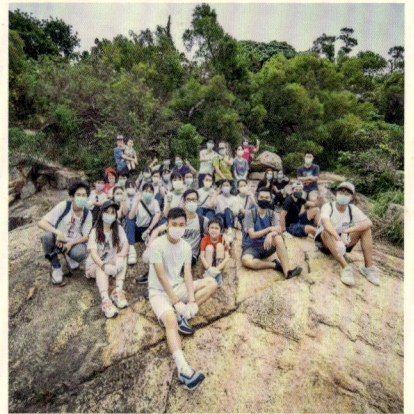

蔡继有书院 守卫地球净滩行动
CKYC's beach clean-up activity

何鸿燊东亚书院 暑期服务学习计划
SEAC's summer service learning programme

郑裕彤书院 贵州从江扶贫服务学习计划
CYTC's service learning trip to Congjiang, Guizhou

4.

文化参与
Cultural engagement

郑裕彤书院 茶文化展示工作坊
CYTC's tea performing workshop

蔡继有书院 文艺探索项目
CKYC's art and culture exploration programme

张昆仑书院 中华文化考察学习系列
CKLC's Chinese culture study trip series

曹光彪书院 和谐粉彩绘画体验项目
CKPC's pastel nagomi art painting programme

何鸿燊东亚书院 乐施会留守儿童艺术展
SEAC's Oxfam left-behind children exhibition

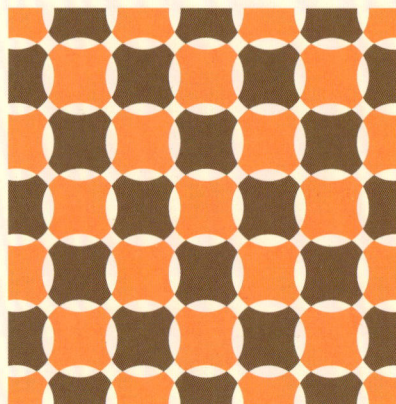

霍英东珍禧书院 参观艺术展览项目
FPJC's visit to art exhibition programme

张昆仑书院 艺文系列
CKLC's art and culture series

蔡继有书院 传统粤剧表演项目
CKYC's traditional cantonese opera performance

满珍纪念书院 音乐卓越项目
MCMC's music excellence programme

绍邦书院 合唱和谐·艺术真谛项目
SPC's vocal harmony programme

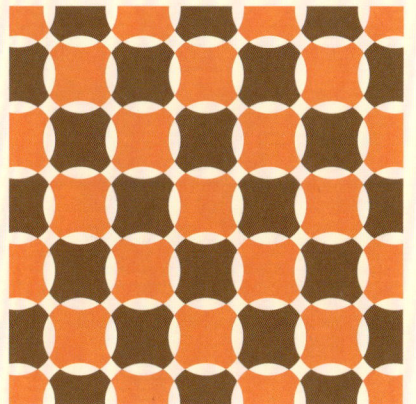

5.

健康生活
Healthy living

吕志和书院 篮球队项目
LCWC's basketball programme

曹光彪书院 运动攀登课程
CKPC's climbing programme

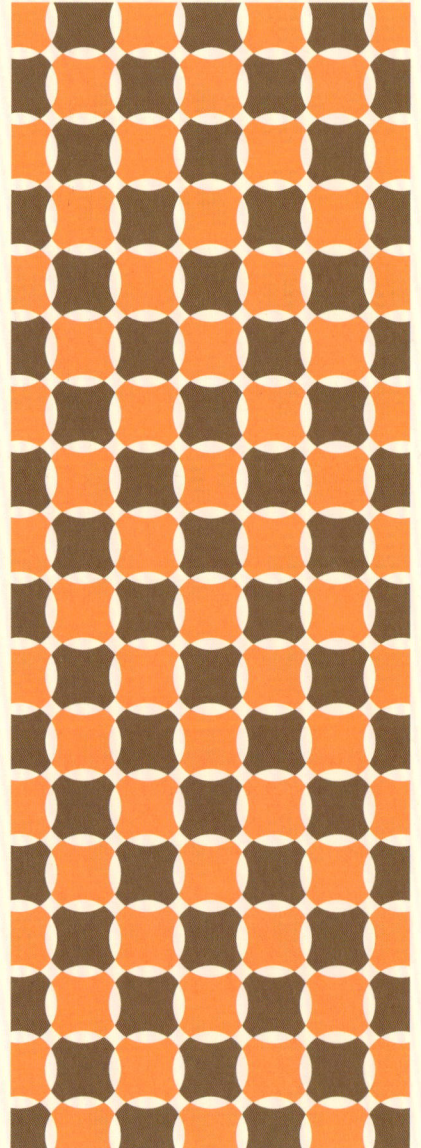

满珍纪念书院 语言能力，心理健康项目
MCMC's language skills and mental health programme

马万祺罗柏心书院 强健体魄项目
MLC's sports programme

何鸿燊东亚书院 走近大自然项目
SEAC's a walk in nature programme

曹光彪书院路环秘境探索项目
CKPC's Coloane rock beach adventure programme

马万祺罗柏心书院 足球队项目
MLC's football programme

自全面实施书院教育以来，澳大经历了五六年必经的摸索之路，将其他地方书院的先进经验，逐步转化落实到澳大新校区，让这种以育人为主的教化环境，慢慢植根于澳门特区的社会土壤。草创期的首要之务，就是建立起一套有效的育人机制，对住宿生起到培养气质、陶冶品格的作用。在这个阶段，为了聚焦于建立通过社群生活来育人的制度，书院集中进行课堂以外的品格教育，学院则集中在课堂教授学术内容。两者明确分工，各司其职。在这个制度框架下，书院在育人方面的制度建设以及实践，可谓取得了阶段性的重要成果，奠定了澳大书院育人的基础，累积了宝贵的经验，也培训了一支专业而有经验的教学及管理骨干队伍。澳大书院系统曾使用不同评估工具，进行初步评估调查。调查发现，相关人员经常在各种内部及外部的教育平台进行交流，不断检讨及改进。部分调查结果亦已发表，可参考本书的附录。总体上，可以看到澳大的书院生活体验，对学生产生了积极的教育作用，并且获得高等教育界正面的评价。

Since its full implementation, UM's RC system has undergone an arduous and fruitful journey of exploration in the past five to six years. With relentless efforts, the university introduced a transformed RC system drawn from extensive experience of overseas universities, transplanted and implemented our own version at UM's new campus. Thus, the enriching educational environment centring with students' all-round development at its core started to take shape and gradually took root in the soil of the Macao community. In the early stage, the primary mission was to establish an effective nurturing mechanism for shaping the temperament and cultivating the character of the students living in the RCs. In this stage, in order to develop a system of education through community life, the RCs were mainly tasked to carry out character education outside the classroom, while the faculties focused on imparting academic knowledge in a classroom setting. The two had distinctive and separate functions and purposes. Based on this framework, major achievements were made in the establishment and implementation of an educational framework for the nurturing of students in the RC system. The RCs laid a good foundation, generated valuable experience and trained a professional as well as experienced team of academic and management staff. The RC system in UM had undergone preliminary assessments using different assessment tools. RC-related staff participated in various internal and external education platforms to exchange ideas, and conducted self-reviews for continual improvement. Some of their studies were published as listed in the appendix of this book. All in all, it is evident that the experience of living in the RCs of UM produced a positive edifying effect on students and received acclaim from the higher education sector.

发展与优化时期的
澳大住宿式书院

Development and Enhancement Phase
of UM Residential College Education

第七章

理念及设施

　　澳大书院制自 2014 年全面实施后，第一批学生在 2018 年秋季毕业。澳大领导层对书院的运作进行了较全面的反思和检讨。2019 年开始，在书院试行及实践时期的基础和经验之上，同时配合新一届特区政府的施政方针，国家有关粤港澳大湾区的发展规划，以及响应特区政府对澳大培育爱国、爱澳而又具全球竞争力人才的殷切期许，澳大与时俱进，通过凝聚共识，精心设计，开启了书院后草创阶段的发展，由试行及实践期成长为发展与优化期，迈向新的里程碑，助力推动"一国两制"行稳致远。

　　2020—2021 学年起，书院开始循序渐进地向新的教育目的优化方向出发，以期取得新的教育成果。首先，书院首要核心的教育成果，是培养出有责任心的公民。良好公民的基本素质，包括具有家国情怀、奉公守法、廉洁诚信、服务社会等。其次，书院必要的教育成果，是培养出品学兼备且具有国际竞争力的大学毕业生，所以需要系统化地加强书院在学术方面的教育功能，不分课堂内外，学习与生活需有机结合。书院要为学生的专业教育、通识教育、研究实习等三方面，提供更有效的辅导及全面支持。更重要的是发挥书院与学院的协同效应，为学生创造多学科、多文化的交流协作环境和提供更多经验，提升他们在学业和事业上的竞争力。最后，发展与优化时期的教育新特色是明确七大胜任力的培养，即公民责任心、全球竞争力、知识整合能力、团队协作、服务与领导、文化参与和健康生活。这七大胜任力，相辅相成，构成全人教育。但最终仍要为首要核心的教育成果服务，即旨在培育有心有力的好公民。有心的心，是好公民好市民之心；有力之力，是在澳门、湾区、全国、国际的竞争力。学识与品格，不可或缺。合则两利，离则俱弊。

书院鼓励学生保持积极的人生态度及健康生活观
RCs encourage students to have a positive attitude and healthy lifestyle.

住宿式书院的正门景观
Main entrance of a RC

　　在上述的理念之下，澳大书院既是社群教育的重要机制，又是一个综合性的学习平台，书院住宿生来自不同专业背景，营造了充满启发性的环境，让大家得以互相学习，增广见闻，并且学习如何与不同专业的人共存共处、合作互助，借以了解毕业后真实的社会环境。此外，书院有驻院及非驻院学术导师，除提供个人指导以外，亦开设可自由参加的学术导修课，包括专业课、通识课以及专业外语课等，体现了澳大"四位一体"的全人教育理念，目的是力求培养学有所成、慎思明辨、情操高尚的大学毕业生。

　　发展与优化时期的书院在设施方面，有两大优化计划：加建楼层及优化膳食制度。由于学生人数增加，本科生人数近年已超过 7000。同时，占 70% 以上的本地本科生的宿位需求亦不断上升，故此有必要增加书院的宿位数目。由于校园可供发展的空间已经不多，最具经济效益的做法无疑是在现存十间书院之上，增建楼层。此项目由校园原设计者何镜堂院士团队承办，在不妨碍校园整体景观的前提之下，在各书院增建少量楼层。该项目自 2021 年暑期开始，计划在五年内完成，届时将增加 1000 多个宿位，使入宿比率提升至比较理想的八成左右。

　　食堂规模维持不变，但运作模式做出了优化，由原来的承包餐制度，改革为市场导向的餐饮服务，并由澳大提供共膳参与津贴，以鼓励住宿生在所属书院共膳，达到同宿共膳的目的，营造书院社群的教化氛围，增强书院学习平台的育人功能。期待新制度为招标带来新机，可以让更多高品质的澳门中小餐饮企业投标，让学生有更多选择，在书院有更好的膳食体验。

Chapter 7

Concept and Facilities

UM's RCs were fully implemented in 2014, with the first cohort of students having graduated in the fall of 2018. At this juncture, the university leadership could reflect on and review the operation of the RCs in a more holistic manner.

Since 2019, based on the the previous trial run and implementation experience of RC education, and in line with the policy objectives of the new Macao SAR administration, the development plan of the Greater Bay Area, and the SAR's expectations for the university to nurture patriotic and globally competitive talents, the university has moved ahead and initiated the second stage for the development of its RCs. Through consensus building and careful design, it has upgraded the initial RC trial run experience to further development and enhancement, striding towards a new milestone and further commitment to the stable and long-term development of the "One Country, Two Systems" constitutional framework in the Macao SAR.

Beginning in academic year 2020−2021, the RCs have started implementing the newly updated educational goals in a progressive manner, with the aim of achieving new educational outcomes. Firstly, the primary educational goal of the RCs is the cultivation of responsible citizenship. The essential qualities of a responsible citizen include love for the home country, law-abidance, integrity, and service to the community among others. Secondly, a necessary educational outcome of the RCs is a university graduate with global competitiveness. Therefore, there is a need to systematically strengthen the RCs' academic role both inside and outside the classroom, and to integrate learning with daily college life in a holistic manner. The RCs are expected to provide more effective guidance and comprehensive support for students in three components of their academic studies: disciplinary education, general education, and research or internship. More importantly, it is necessary to strengthen the synergy between the RCs and the faculties so as to provide an overall environment conductive to

书院鼓励学生通过与不同专业的同学协作交流，提升解决问题和沟通的能力
RCs encourage student to improve their problem-solving and communication skills by collaborating with classmates from different majors or disciplines.

multi-disciplinary and multi-cultural interchange as well as collaborative learning, thereby enhancing students' competitiveness in their studies and careers. Thirdly, the development and enhancement phase of RU education is characterised by its encapsulation of its education outcomes into seven competencies, namely: responsible citizenship, global competitiveness, knowledge integration, teamwork and collaboration, service and leadership, cultural engagement, and healthy lifestyle. The seven competencies of RC are complementary to each other, and jointly form the attributes of whole person development. Together, these competencies serve its core — the nurturing of responsible citizens with global competitiveness, that is a person with a strong sense of responsibility and competent, and knowledgeable to be competitive locally, regionally, nationally, and internationally. They must possess good knowledge and character at the same time. These two qualities of good knowledge and good character are mutually reinforcing, and a responsible citizen with global competitiveness should possess both qualities.

This being the case, the UM's RCs are not only an important mechanism for community and peer education, but also an integrative learning platform. Students from different academic disciplines living together create a stimulating learning environment where they learn from each other, broaden their horizons, and get to know how to co-exist and cooperate with people from various academic backgrounds. This provides a glimpse into real-life situations after their graduation. In addition, each RC has resident and non-resident fellows who provide personal guidance and run non-credit-bearing and optional tutorials pertaining to disciplinary studies, general education, and academic language skills. This embodies the 4-in-1 educational model of whole-person education promoted by the university. The aim is to produce university graduates who are academically accomplished and of high moral standard.

The education during the development and enhancement phase has two major enhancements in terms of facilities and operations: the construction of additional floors and the improvement of the dining system. The number of undergraduates has surpassed 7,000 in recent years, due to growth in student population. Concurrently, the demand for accommodation for local undergraduates, who account for over 70 percent of the student population, is also on the rise. It is therefore necessary to increase the accommodation capacity in the RCs. As free open physical space is becoming scarce on the campus, the most economically efficient way is undoubtedly to build additional floors on top of the 10 existing RCs. The project has invited Professor He Jingtang, the original architect of the campus, and his team to be the design team. The aim is to build a small number of additional floors in each college, without compromising the overall campus landscape and ecology. Starting in the summer of 2021, the project is scheduled to be completed in five years. By then, more than 1,000 additional bedspace will be made available; this brings the occupancy rate to 80 percent, an ideal target addressing the needs of UM's students.

The communal meal function of the dining halls remains unchanged, but their mode of operation has been optimised, from the former rigid system of basic meal provision to a more flexible and market-oriented catering service, with the university providing a communal meal allowance to encourage students to dine together collegiately in their respective RCs. The aim is to create an educational environment in the RC community and enhance their nurturing role as a learning platform through communal dining. It is expected that the new system will bring new opportunities for tendering, allowing more high-quality local food small and medium enterprises (SME) to bid, increasing choice for students, and optimising their dining experience in the RCs.

书院岛二区景致
The landscape of RC Island Two

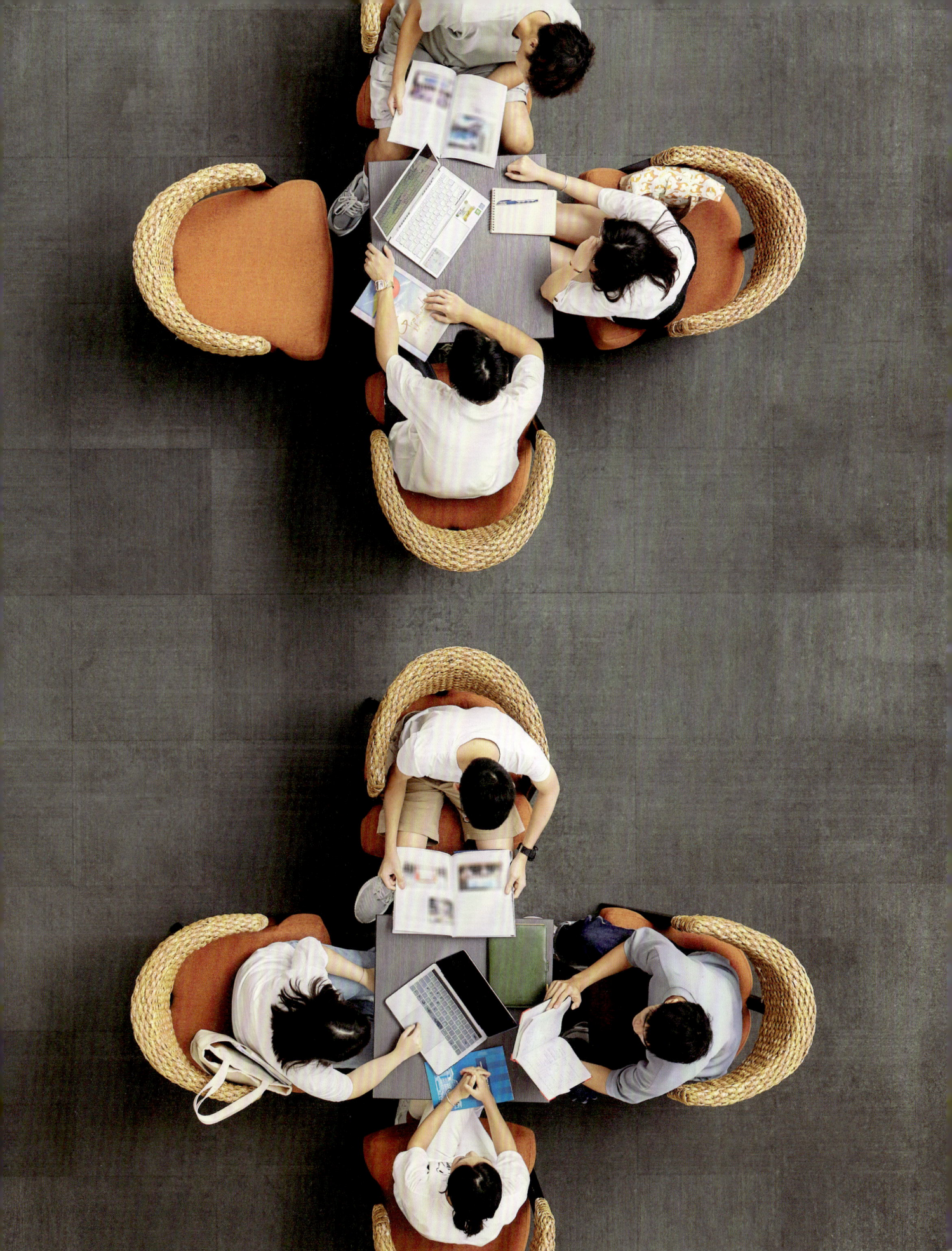

澳门大学图书馆的学习共享空间
Learning commons in University of Macau Library

第八章

教育机制及组织

为配合前述的优化方向，书院试行了以下一系列新教育机制。

书院学术导修制度：经过 2019—2020 学年的试行，从 2020—2021 学年开始，书院将全面推行学术导修班制，不设学分，学生可自由参与，每班十人至二十人不等，主要由书院的驻院或非驻院导师任教或进行指导。导师辅导课程分为主修科学术导修班及通识科学术导修班两大类。主修科学术导修班暂时分为三类：一是高级学术研讨导修班，由资深教师主持，阅读及准备工作要求极高，学生自愿参加，但必须积极阅读材料和参与讨论。二是普通学术知识或方法培训导修班，由专业教师设计及指导，学生互相协同进行团队式学习，并受训成为培训员，推广同内容导修班。三是双语主修导修班，专为来自中文教育背景的学生而设，帮助他们适应使用英语教授的主修科目，如生命科学等，由驻院或非驻院的专业背景教师主持。此外，为有需要的学生设学术英语导修班，加强学术英语培训。

在教师方面，一方面，澳大要求驻院教学人员成为学院或学系的正式老师，在适当情况下参与教授专业或通识课程；另一方面，亦鼓励学院或学系老师在书院的专业教育或通识教育上，扮演更重要的角色。凡此种种，皆为学业与品格相融合的四位一体教育，奠定了制度的基础。

住宿式书院内的阅读及学习空间
Reading and learning space in RCs

来自各地的学生住在住宿式书院有助于文化交流
Students from all over the world living together in RCs, which facilitates cultural exchange.

"书院体验式学习"（RC Experiential Learning）课程及书院要求的优化：从 2020-2021 学年开始，优化后的 1 学分社群教育必修课程——"书院体验式学习"，明确了新的预期学习成果，与书院活动等的要求相互协调，重新整合，协助大一新生适应大学学习模式和生活，以打造就业导向的个人电子履历档案为手段，指导学生有效计划四年的大学生活，为参与重要的活动保留深刻反思的文字纪录，呈现个人成长的历程，凸显学生的品格素质，提升事业竞争力，并为终身事业做出长期规划。

另外，设立了一门 1 学分社群教育必修课程——"书院社区团队项目"(RC Community Team Project)。从 2021 年入学的学生开始，所有学生需在二年级时修完"书院社区团队项目"课程。此项目的目的是通过向社会推广特定的正面价值观或信息，进行创意团队服务，并且通过主动学习及体验式学习，让学生发挥及运用其多元学术专业和专长，更深刻地活用相关的价值观与信息，同时增加对社会的了解，建立社区网络，实践团队协作，提升个

人在大湾区内外的事业竞争力。项目主题分八个价值范畴，初拟为家国情怀、遵纪守法、廉洁诚信、社会责任、人际关系、服务他人、文化传承、积极人生。这些范畴每年会进行增删。每个范畴各有三个主题区域，共二十四个主题区域，也可每年进行调整。学生团队从二十四个主题区域内选定各队的主题区域。各队在主题区域内，选定具有重要正面信息的具体主题，并选择受众，如中小学生、老年人等，然后进行集体创作，以最有效的方式把信息传递给选定的受众，借以提升社会整体素质。这体现了该项目的宗旨——社会服务，也是学生团队具体的工作。团队最后需要做口头报告，包括整个团队活动的过程介绍、反省以及个人感受。报告可以用作各同学个人电子履历档案的主要事例之一。

关顾辅导及思想价值观工作的强化：书院必须为所有住宿生分配至少一位书院教学人员为其大学生活的指导老师，定期面谈，建立点对点的个人沟通渠道和互信，进行关顾辅导和价值观、政治观方面的思想教育工作。每位学生干部必须领导至少一

个住宿生小组，协助书院学术导师提供同侪关顾服务。在新方向下，书院教学、行政人员及学生干部，需接受有关关顾辅导及调解技巧的基本培训。此外，心理辅导处每周会分派兼职辅导员到各间书院，为有需要的学生提供专业的心理辅导。同时，亦为书院师生安排辅导基础知识培训，如心理健康护理初级班、冲突调解处理技巧班等。

打造"四位一体"全人教育的多学科综合实践平台：优化后的"书院体验式学习"课程和"书院社区团队项目"课程，训练学生如何把在学院学到的专业知识和通识知识活学活用，融入多文化、多学科的书院环境，学习和不同专业及背景的院生沟通及交流，通过多元团队合作而发挥协同效应。这些将会贯彻书院生活的各个方面。

书院组织方面，早在 2017 年秋，澳大就对书院系统的管理架构及财政模式进行反思，并实施新的制度。其要点为：一是加强澳大在书院管治架构上的督导职能，在发挥个别书院特色及精神之余，使书院系统作为一个有机整体运作及呈现多元一体的问责格局。二是加强对书院的财务管理，增加成本效益，更好地落实公共资金使用上的监督问责。三是加强书院与学院的联系，设立共三学分的三门社群教育必修课程。并重新界定学院教师作为书院导师的身份与职能，扩大了书院的非驻院导师团队。四是优化书院行政人员编制，提升管理效率。新制度由 2018 年 1 月开始施行。从 2021 年起，驻院教学人员陆续成为学院或学系的正式老师，但其主要工作仍然是推行书院教育。

书院组织各种活动培养学生建立良好的人际关系，提升沟通技巧
RCs organise various activities to cultivate students' good interpersonal relationships and improve their communication skills.

Chapter 8

Education Programmes and Organisation

书院组织活动加强外语能力，提升跨文化沟通技巧
RCs organise activities to strengthen students' foreign language and inter-cultural communication skills.

At the heart of the changes under the development and enhancement phase of RC education is the enhancement of the educational role and curricula of the RCs, thus the RCs will pilot the following new education programmes.

RC academic tutorials: After a trial run in the academic year 2019－2020, the RCs fully implemented the academic tutorial programme starting from 2020－2021. These non-credit-bearing, optional tutorials are taught or supervised by the RCs' resident and non-resident fellows, conducted in small groups of 10 to 20 students in each session. The tutorials are categorised into academic disciplinary tutorials and general education tutorials. At this pilot stage, the discipline-based academic tutorials are of the following three types: (a) Advanced-level academic tutorials, conducted by senior academic staff and entailing intensive reading and preparation. The students participate on a voluntary basis but must be proactive in completing reading assignments and taking part in discussions. (b) General-level tutorials on academic knowledge or methodology, designed and supervised by professors in the respective discipline, where students collaborate in team learning and are trained to become trainers themselves for future tutorials in the same subject. (c) Bilingual academic majors tutorials, designed to help students from Chinese-speaking schools adapt to English-language instruction in their major subjects that are taught in English, such as life sciences, and are conducted by resident or non-resident academic staff from the relevant field. Academic English tutorials are also available to provide academic English training for students in need.

In terms of academic staff, on one hand, the university requires resident academic staff of the RCs to be officially affiliated with faculties and departments and to teach credit-bearing courses in the faculties where appropriate. On the other hand, it also encourages teaching staff from the faculties and departments to play a greater role in tutorials or academic advising in the RCs. All of these arrangements reinforce the institutional foundation for the 4-in-1 education model that integrates academic studies with character cultivation.

书院学习氛围鼓励学生发挥创意，提升知识整合能力
Students are encouraged to be creative to enhance their knowledge integration ability.

Enhancing the RC Experiential Learning course and RC requirements: Starting from academic year 2020 – 2021, the 1-credit compulsory community and peer education course — RC Experiential Learning has a new set of intended learning outcomes. Reintegrated and working in conjunction with other RC requirements such as RC activities, the new course helps first-year students adapt to university learning and college life. It guides students to build their own career-oriented e-portfolios. By means of building a career-oriented e-portfolio, students learn to plan for their four years of university life and keep records of their reflections on major events that they participated in. The career-oriented-e-portfolio will document milestones of students' personal growth, highlight their characters and personal qualities, improve their professional competitiveness and serve as a tool for their life-long career planning.

Another 1-credit compulsory community and peer education course — RC Community Team Project will also be introduced. From the cohort of 2021, all new students are required to fulfil this RC requirement by the end of their second year. This course requires students to promote specified positive values or messages in the community through a creative community service team project. Through active learning and experiential learning, they have the chance to collaborate using their expertise and the knowledge acquired in their different academic majors to explore those values and messages thoroughly. It also enables them to deepen their understanding of the society, build community networks, practise teamwork and elevate their professional competitiveness within and outside the Greater Bay Area. The project scope centres around one of the following eight values, which are preliminarily set as follows: love for one's home country, law-abidance, integrity and honesty, social responsibility, interpersonal relations, service

to others, cultural preservation and positive attitude. These values are reviewed every year and subject to revision when needed. Three topic areas will be set under each value, making a total of 24 topic areas which are also subject to adjustment, addition and deletion annually. Each student team selects one topic area and determines a specific topic therein that carries important positive messages. They then work collectively to deliver the messages to the target audience of their choice such as primary and secondary school students, elderly people, using the most effective electronic means, thus promoting positive social values of the community. This intended outcome reflects the purpose of this community service project and is also the specific focus of the task of the student teams. Finally, each team is required to give an oral presentation documenting the whole process, and reflection on personal feelings. The report can be included as an entry in students' career-oriented-e-portfolios.

Strengthening pastoral care and positive values education: Each RC student must be assigned at least one RC academic staff member as mentor throughout their university years. Individual meetings will be held on a regular basis to develop mutual trust and person-to-person communication upon which emotional care and cultivation of moral and civic values can be delivered. Each student leader is required to take care of one group of RC students providing peer support in addition to that provided by the academic staff. Under this new direction, academic staff, administrative staff and student leaders of the RCs need to go through basic training in counselling and mediation. In addition, part-time counsellors are assigned weekly to each RC by the Student Counselling Section so as to provide professional counselling for those students in need.

RC as a multi-disciplinary platform for knowledge integration and application, embodying the ideal of whole-person development in the 4-in-1 education model: The two enhanced compulsory courses, RC Experiential Learning and RC Community Team Project, train students to creatively apply knowledge acquired from academic majors and general education in the real-life, multi-cultural and multi-disciplinary environment of the RCs. They will learn how to communicate and work with students from different majors and backgrounds and how to achieve synergy through teamwork. This inclusive learning mindset will permeate through every aspect of their RC life.

In terms of RC organisation, as early as in the fall of 2017, the university reviewed the management structure and financial model of the RC system and made systematic enhancements including the following: (a) Reinforcing the university's oversight of the RC system's governance structure, while promoting diversity in respective characteristics and spirits of each RC, ensures the smooth operation of the RC system as an organic whole with an integrated accountability framework that reflects diversity. (b) Strengthening the university's management of the RCs' financial matters, improving cost effectiveness and ensuring effective monitoring and accountability of the use of public funds. (c) Deepening the connection between the RCs and the faculties, setting up three compulsory community and peer education courses with a total of three credits, and redefining the roles and duties of academic staff of faculties serving as fellows or affiliates in the RCs, thereby expanding the non-resident fellowship. (d) Streamlining the arrangement of administrative staff to improve efficiency. The systematic enhancements were introduced in January 2018. Starting from 2021, RC academic staff have gradually become official members of faculties and departments with various degrees of involvement in teaching and research, although their main duties remain the delivering of education in RC programmes and activities.

文化参与是书院教育其中一个重点培育的胜任力
Cultural engagement is one of the key competencies promoted in RC education.

第九章

住宿式书院发展与优化时期七大胜任力教育

胜任力既是一种技能，建基于达到胜任水平的知识或技巧；也是一股行动力量，从价值观和感情认同中自动产生。作为书院教育成果的七大胜任力，各有四种品格属性，可以作为定性或定量检测的对象。四种品格均相辅相成，互相增益，形成完整的胜任力。

1. 公民责任心

- **家国情怀：**公民最基本的责任是怀抱家国之情。对中国澳门本地学生而言，即爱国、爱澳之情。对非澳门本地的中国学生而言，爱国之外，可怀有以澳门为第二故乡之情。国际学生除热爱自己的祖国及家乡之外，亦可怀有以澳门为第二故乡之情。家国情怀，同时应建基于对家国的认同和了解之上。
- **社会责任感：**公民对自己所处的社会，应自觉地肩负各种社会责任，并主动承担社会义务。
- **遵纪守法：**公民的基本责任之一，即对所处社会的法律有基本的认识，并且主动遵守法纪，维护法纪。对于中国澳门本地学生而言，首要的就是对《中华人民共和国宪法》和《中华人民共和国澳门特别行政区基本法》的学习、认知和遵守。
- **廉洁诚信：**贪污腐败、枉法欺诈会对社会造成莫大的破坏。有责任心的公民应对有关廉洁及诚信的法律和道德规范有基本的认识，并且主动遵守和推广。

2. 全球竞争力

- **国际视野：**不论大小的社会、政治、经济、文化等议题，不论涉及国内或国际，都可以从全球角度出发，加以思考。学生养成从国际视野思考所有重要问题的习惯，是提高全球竞争力的基石。
- **跨文化沟通：**自觉加强外语能力，对不同的文化持开放态度，努力追求更深入的了解，借以进行有效的跨文化沟通。这是提高全球竞争力的起点。
- **包容多元文化：**对其他文化保持尊重和包容的态度，能欣赏各种不同的文化，是维持全球竞争力的要素。
- **自主自强：**具有独立思辨和自主决策的动机及能力，始能自强不息，始能在全球竞争中不被淘汰。

3. 知识整合能力

- **融会贯通学术知识：**学术知识日新月异，网络时代知识爆炸，若不能融会贯通，极可能仅是博览，而不知旨要。各种知识的融通，既是应该追求的价值，也是必须培养的能力。
- **跨学科沟通、协作及应用：**现代社会使用知识解决问题时，往往需要不同专业间的协力合作，因此能与其他专业人士顺畅沟通，互相合作而创造协同效应，将是应用知识做大事、办要务的必要条件。
- **批判思维：**在百家齐放、众说纷纭、信息泛滥、真假难辨的网络时代，认识批判力的重要性，并尽力增强这方面的能力，始能去芜存菁，不致随波逐流。明辨真假是非黑白，才能谈到有效知识的整合和应用。
- **创意创新：**社会进步，唯靠新知。脱颖而出，端赖创意。知识整合有助催生想象，知识整合有助跨界探索，知识整合有助打破成见。知识整合既是创意的基础，又是创新的动力。

学生除了参与书院举办的活动，也需要自发组织活动把课堂里学到的能力应用于实践
Students are required to organise activities and apply what they have learned in RCs.

书院为学生提供参与各种体育活动的机会
RCs provide opportunities for students to participate in various sports activities.

书院重视培养学生的团队精神、归属感和认同感并在日常生活加强师生沟通工作
RCs emphasise the importance of cultivating students' team spirit, sense of belonging, and strengthening the communication between teachers and students in daily life.

4. 团队协作

- **人际关系：** 在团队或集体生活中，良好的人际关系不仅是成事之要素，而且也是个人快乐之泉源。如何处理负面的人际关系，如何调解冲突，处理矛盾，亦是形成良好人际关系的要件。建立良好人际关系既是应有的价值观，也是一种适应社会环境的能力。
- **团队协力：** 团队内部齐心协力，能量往往远超个别成员能力的总和。能认识并坚持这种价值观，并掌握付诸实行之道，对事业成功和幸福至为重要。
- **队际合作：** 团队之间的竞争虽可带来进步，但竞争必须良性双赢，否则成果不易持久，文明难以赓续。团队之间倘能合作，效果亦可超越个别团队能量总和，双赢之外，可以增进社会整体利益。跨团队合作，既是人生的态度，也体现做人的能力。
- **团队精神：** 团队贵在集体精神。其成员对团队的认同感、归属感，是团队成功的基础。团体成功，团体精神强盛，其成员亦能分享成功的果实。了解团队精神的重要性，并且掌握培养团队精神的方法，将是衡量团队协作胜任力的重要指标。

5. 服务与领导

- **战略思维：** 领导之责在高瞻远瞩，领导之本在服务社会。处处从大局着想，事事循大处入手。以服务为本的领导力，必从战略思维出发，然后方能达到领导的目的。
- **服务他人：** 以服务为本的领导，建基于助人以诚、服务为乐的态度，并由此催生出学习相关知识技巧的动力。
- **组织能力：** 轻重先后，有条不紊；分工立例，各司其职。效率由此提高，纷争庶几稍息。良好的组织能力，既是一种向往的价值追求，也是胜任领导的条件。
- **以身作则：** 上行下效，自古皆然。领导者贵在自发成为榜样。律己从严，待人以宽。服务为本的领导，尤当如是。

6. 文化参与

- **文化修养：** 文化修养体现在知识、技能的习得，也建基于热诚和向往。自觉地对一些文化知识和实践抱有感兴趣、热情和欣赏的态度，愿意投入心血和时间，以获得相关的修养，是文化参与胜任力的根本。
- **文化传承：** 尊重和保护不同的文化，对热爱的文化，怀抱着加以保护、继承和发扬光大的理想。
- **文化创意：** 有文化创造的冲动，对从事文化创意活动表示喜爱、满足和有成就感。对他人的文化创意成果，能够尊重、欣赏和理解。
- **文化自信：** 在尊重和欣赏其他国家文化时，对自己国家的文化尤其感到自信和自豪。中国学生必须以学习、保护、传承和传播中华优秀传统文化为己任。

7. 健康生活

- **健康饮食：** 积极吸收有关健康饮食的知识，并持之以恒地付诸实践。
- **积极人生：** 保持积极的人生观，增强抗逆力，以助人为快乐之本，为促进他人、群体及社会的幸福而努力。
- **强身健体：** 积极吸收有关日常运动的正确知识，并持之以恒地实践，方能维持健康体魄，并以此为日常生活的基本方式。
- **环保意识：** 积极了解环保的知识和责任，持之以恒地付诸实践及推广，并且将其作为健康生活的一个重要指标。

Chapter 9

Seven Competencies of RC Education during the Development and Enhancement Phase

On one hand, competencies refer to skills when a certain level of dexterity or knowledge has been attained; on the other hand, competencies also refer to personal values or traits which motivate one's actions. The seven competencies constitute the expected outcome of the education under RC education during the development and enhancement phase. Each of them consists of four attributes, which can be assessed qualitatively or quantitatively. The four attributes, complementing and reinforcing one another, comprise the essential aspects of the competency. A brief description of each attribute of these competencies is given as follows.

学生在尊重和欣赏其他国家的文化时，学习传播中华传统文化
Students learn to spread traditional Chinese culture while respecting and appreciating the cultures of other countries.

1. Responsible citizenship

- **Affection for home country:** The most fundamental responsibility of a citizen is patriotism. For local Chinese students in Macao, it means love for the country and Macao. For non-local Chinese students, apart from love for the country, they may have affection for Macao as their second hometown. As for international students, they may regard Macao as their second hometown, in addition to respect and love for their own country and hometown. Affection for one's home country should be built on one's identification with and understanding of the country.
- **Social responsibility:** Citizens should voluntarily shoulder social responsibilities in the society where they live, and assume their own social obligations.
- **Law-abidance:** One of the basic responsibilities of a citizen is to have a basic knowledge of the laws of the society where one lives, and to consciously observe and uphold the law. For local Chinese students in Macao, the first priority is to learn, understand and abide by the Constitution of the People's Republic of China and the Basic Law of the Macao Special Administrative Region of the People's Republic of China.
- **Integrity:** Corruption, abuse of the law and fraud would cause immeasurable damage to society. A responsible citizen should also have a general understanding of the legal and ethical dimensions of integrity and honesty, as opposite to corruption and deception, and actively comply and promulgate them.

2. Global competitiveness

- **Global perspective:** Social, political, economic, cultural and other issues, whether large or small, be it local or international, can be approached from a global perspective. Developing the habit of thinking about all important matters from a global perspective is the cornerstone for students to build global competitiveness.
- **Intercultural communication:** Students should realise the need to strengthen their foreign language skills, be open to different cultures and strive for a deeper understanding of them, in order to engage in effective cross-cultural communication. This is the starting point towards global competitiveness.
- **Cultural inclusiveness:** Respect and tolerance for cultures different from one's own as well as the ability to appreciate them is an essential element in maintaining global competitiveness.
- **Independence and self-motivation:** With the motivation and capacity to think and make decisions independently, students will be able to continuously improve themselves and thrive in global competition.

3. Knowledge integration

- **Integration of academic knowledge:** Academic knowledge is advancing rapidly and growing exponentially in the Internet era. If students lack the skills to integrate and harness what they have learnt in different domains of knowledge, they may end up being overloaded with fragmentary knowledge, despite extensive reading. As a result, they could be left with abundant unconnected information with little insight of what such information implies. The ability to integrate and connect various kinds of knowledge is not only a value worth pursuing, but also an indispensable ability in the information era.
- **Interdisciplinary communication, collaboration, and application:** The use of knowledge to solve problems in modern society often requires collaboration across different disciplines. Therefore, the ability to communicate smoothly and effectively with professionals in other sectors with a view of creating synergy is a necessary condition for application of knowledge in handling important affairs.
- **Critical thinking:** In the age of the Internet, where there are so many different voices and opinions and so much information that is difficult to separate fact from fiction, students should recognise the importance of analytical and critical thinking and do their best to strengthen their capability in this regard. Only in this way will they be able to distinguish what is valuable or useful from what is worthless and useless, and avoid blindly falling in with the crowd. Only when one can distinguish truth from falsehood and able to garner essential information, can one effectively integrate and apply knowledge.
- **Creativity and innovation:** Social progress is possible only with new knowledge and breakthrough achievements springing from creativity. Knowledge integration is conducive to inspiring imagination, cross-disciplinary exploration and thinking out of the box. It is the foundation of creativity as well as a driving force for innovation.

4. Teamwork and collaboration

- **Interpersonal relationships:** Good interpersonal relationships, in a team or in communal life, are not only the key to success, but also a source of personal happiness. Knowing how to smooth out negative personal relationships and how to mediate conflicts and resolve disputes is also an intrinsic part of strong interpersonal skills. Skill in maintaining good interpersonal relationships is not only a desirable trait but it also demonstrates an ability to cope with social environment effectively.
- **Collaborative teamwork:** The power of a team working together is often much greater than the sum of its individual members' capabilities. Recognising and embracing this idea, and knowing how to put it into practice, are essential to one's career and happiness.
- **Cross-team cooperation:** Competition between teams can bring progress; but it must be of a healthy, win-win nature, instead of a fight to the bitter end. Otherwise, the progress achieved would not be easily sustained and, by extension, would make it difficult for civilisations to survive. If teams can collaborate with each other, the synergy will be greater than the sum of the energy of individual teams. In addition to achieving a win-win situation, it can add to the overall benefit of society. Cooperation across teams embodies an attitude of life as well as the ability to engage with people.
- **Team spirit:** The beauty of a team lies in its team spirit. Team members' sense of identity and belonging to the team makes the foundation of a successful team. When a team achieves success and the team spirit is strong, its members can also share the fruits of its success. Understanding the importance of team spirit and mastering how to foster it is an important indicator of the competency of teamwork and collaboration.

5. Service and leadership

- **Strategic thinking:** The responsibility of leadership is to look far ahead and aim high while its essence is to serve the community. A leader should always bear the big picture in mind, set the right priority, and focus first on the major issues when handling situations. Acumen and insightfulness are necessary qualities for one to lead others towards common good and make a difference. Service-oriented leadership must be underpinned by strategic thinking in order to achieve the purpose at hand.
- **Service to others:** Service-oriented leadership is based on the sincere desire to help others and derive pleasure therefrom. This desire can strongly motivate one to acquire relevant knowledge and skills.
- **Organisational skills:** Prioritising tasks based on their importance and urgency can keep things in order; division of labour with established rules will enable each person to effectively perform their job. These measures can make for efficiency and reduce conflicts and disputes. Good organisational skills are a desirable capability and a requirement for a competent leader.
- **Leading by example:** Subordinates often follow the example of those above. It is important for leaders to take the initiative to act as role models. They should discipline themselves strictly and treat others generously. This is especially true for service-oriented leadership.

学生通过主题工作坊把学术知识融会贯通
Students integrate academic knowledge through thematic workshops.

书院活动培养学生音乐交流的兴趣
RC activities cultivate students' interest in practising music and exchange.

艺术是书院培养创意的教育举措
Art is a way through which creativity is cultivated in RC education

6. Cultural engagement

- **Cultural cultivation:** Cultural cultivation is not only embodied in the acquisition of knowledge and skills, but also underpinned by enthusiasm and aspiration. A genuine interest in, passion for, and appreciation of certain cultural knowledge and practice, and a willingness to invest effort and time in acquiring cultural literacy, are fundamental to the competency of cultural engagement.
- **Cultural preservation:** Students should respect and cherish different cultures. They should be willing to preserve, carry on, and promote any cultural heritage to which they are devoted.
- **Cultural innovation:** Students are expected to have the impetus for cultural creation and find contentment, satisfaction and a sense of achievement when engaging in these creative activities. They should also respect, and be able to appreciate and understand the creative cultural works of others.
- **Cultural confidence:** While respecting and appreciating the cultures of other countries, students should feel confident about and proud of their own culture. Chinese students must take on the responsibility of learning, preserving, passing on and promoting fine traditional Chinese culture.

7. Healthy lifestyle

- **Healthy diet:** Students need to actively acquire knowledge about healthy diet and regularly follow it so as to maintain a healthy lifestyle as a personal choice.
- **Positive attitude:** Students should have a positive outlook on life and strengthen their resilience in the face of adverse conditions. They should try to help others as a source of happiness and willingly strive to promote the happiness of society, communities and other people.
- **Exercise and sport:** Students should actively acquire correct knowledge about daily physical exercise and practise it regularly, in a bid to remain in good health and make it a routine in their daily life.
- **Environmental awareness:** Students should actively acquire knowledge about environmental protection and understand their responsibility in this aspect. They should practice and promote green concepts regularly, and view environmental conservation as an important aspect of healthy lifestyles for all.

本地和国际生在澳门大学图书馆前合影留念
Local and international students take a group photo in front of University of Macau Library.

第十章

教育绩效评估机制

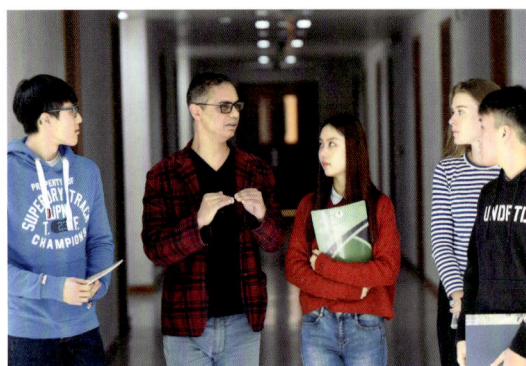

书院教学人员经常与学生交流，观察他们的表现
Academic staff in RCs often communicate with students to observe their performance

今日的澳大书院系统，已经积累了一定的经验，进一步发展出一套相匹配的绩效评估机制，既能达到世界一流高教评估的水平，亦可专业地展示出书院教育的成果。发展与优化时期的澳大书院，一方面，从澳大的经验及澳门的具体情况出发，另一方面，参照国内外先进高教机构的做法，尝试建立了一套长期有效和具有公信力的绩效评估机制。在评估问责之余，亦为书院系统的持续成长与不断优化，提供科学的根据。

发展与优化时期的澳大书院的教育成果检验有三个主要原则：绩效成果与教育目的相匹配（fitness for purpose），教育成果导向的绩效评估（outcome-based approach），教育目标（education objectives）转化为教育成果（education outcome）。教育成果检验包括如下方面。

（1）书院教学人员的年度自我评估工作报告；（2）学生个人电子履历档案数据及分析报告；（3）二年级学生必修"书院社区团队项目"课程的数据库；（4）年度书院学业辅导效果调查；（5）书院课程年度学生意见反馈；（6）年度住宿生心理健康及学习心理状况调查；（7）年度书院公民教育效果调查；（8）年度书院生活对住宿生教育作用调查；（9）年度应届毕业生对书院生活教育作用的反馈调查；（10）离校毕业生追踪调查等。

另外，因应澳大书院的教育成果，利用以上十项数据或其他相关数据，可以设计出下列两项或更多的学生素质综合指数，借以总体掌握书院的教育绩效。（1）学生公民素质综合指数。这项指数旨在评估书院的育人教育成果，检验书院教育在培养家国情怀、奉公守法、廉洁诚信、服务社会等品格素质方面，是否产生可检验及有公信力的绩效。（2）学生竞争力综合指数。这项指数旨在评估书院的竞争力教育成果，检验书院教育在提升学生竞争力，包括专业知识及通识知识的融会贯通、应用实践、跨科协作、创新创业、国际视野、文化热忱、团队合作等素质方面，是否产生可检验及有公信力的绩效。这两种综合指数的部分数据，为前测数据（pre-test data），将在新生入学的第一学期抽样收集。剩余部分数据为后测数据（post-test data），则在毕业前收集，以期对学生在校四年素质增长幅度（added-value），以及书院在素质增长上发挥多少作用做有效评估。

综合制度评估方面，澳大将实行教育绩效五年评估循环机制，即每两年校内各书院及整体书院系统做自评报告；每五年邀请一次校外专家来校做实地检查及提交核证报告。

住宿式书院致力为学生提供优质多元的知识整合平台
RCs are committed to providing students with a high-quality knowledge integration platform.

Chapter 10

Education Performance Assessment

Up to now, UM's RC system has accumulated a certain amount of experience and is in a position to further develop a corresponding performance assessment mechanism that can meet the standards of world-class higher education assessment and scientifically demonstrate the achievements of our RC education. A credible assessment mechanism for RC education during the development and enhancement phase must, on one hand, build on UM's experience and Macao's specific circumstances, while, on the other hand, it must take reference from practices of advanced higher education institutions in China and overseas. It embodies an endeavour to establish a sustainable and credible performance assessment mechanism, which will enable evidence-based continuous advancement of the RC system and serve as an instrument for programme evaluation and accountability.

There are three key principles for gauging the educational outcomes in UM's RC education during the development and enhancement phase: fitness for purpose, outcome-based approach, and realisation of educational objectives as measurable outcomes. The evaluation of the education outcomes comprises, for example, the following measures, among others.

(a) An annual report by RC's teaching staff as a self-assessment exercise; (b) data analysis and report on students' career-oriented-e-portfolio; (c) a database of the compulsory second-year community team projects; (d) annual survey on the effectiveness of academic tutorials in the RCs; (e) student Feedback Questionnaire on the two credit-bearing RC courses; (f) annual survey on mental health and learning attitudes of RC students; (g) annual survey on the effectiveness of citizenship education in the RCs; (h) annual survey on the educational impact of RC life on students; (i) annual survey gathering feedback from fresh graduates on the impact of RC education; (j) alumni tracking survey.

Additionally, in accordance with the educational outcomes of UM's RCs, by using data from the 10 measures above or other similar data, it should be possible to design the following two, or more, composite student quality indexes in order to understand the overall educational performance of the RCs. The first example is student citizenship composite index. This indicator will be designed to measure the outcomes of the RCs' civic education and to test whether the education provided by the RCs has produced verifiable and credible results in developing moral qualities such as love for the home country, law-abidance, integrity, and service to the community, and so on. The second example is student competitiveness composite index. It will be designed to measure the outcomes of the RCs' education regarding competitiveness and to test whether the education provided by the RCs has produced verifiable and credible results in enhancing students' competitiveness including the integration of their major and general knowledge at university level, knowledge application and practice, cross-disciplinary collaboration, innovation and entrepreneurship, global perspective, cultural engagement, teamwork, among others. Some of the data for these two composite indexes consist of pre-test data, which will be collected in the first semester of each new intake. The other part of the data are post-test data, which are collected before graduation, in order to provide a valid assessment on the added-value of the student competencies during their four years of study and the extent to which RCs have contributed to that value.

In terms of comprehensive system review, the university will implement a five-year cycle of evaluation of educational performance. This will include a biennial internal report on the self-evaluation report of each RC and the RC system as a whole, and an external audit report from a team of experts to be invited to the university once every five years to conduct an on-site quality assurance visit.

结　语 / Concluding Remarks

　　由 2020 年秋起，澳大书院踏入发展与优化时期。书院首要的教育成果，是培育有责任心的公民。书院必要的教育成果，是培育具有全球竞争力的大学毕业生。书院的新特色，是以七大胜任力为目标成果的书院教育，即公民责任心、全球竞争力、知识整合能力、团队协作、服务与领导、文化参与和健康生活。以此为教育成果指标，澳大将推行一系列的书院教育举措，以期达到预期的书院教育成果，并且设计了一系列相应的多元化绩效检验机制，借以确认书院的教育理念得以有效落实，以期成为书院教育制度中一个具有参考价值的实践经验。

Starting in autumn 2020, UM's RCs entered their development and enhancement phase. The RCs' primary educational outcome is responsible citizenship. The necessary educational outcomes of the RCs are university graduates with global competitiveness. The RCs' new feature lies in the RC education with the seven competencies as the target outcomes. These include responsible citizenship, global competitiveness, knowledge integration, teamwork and collaboration, service and leadership, cultural engagement, and healthy lifestyle. Using these as indicators of the educational results, the university will implement a series of RC educational initiatives, with a view to achieving the desired outcomes. The university will also develop a series of multi-faceted performance assessment mechanisms to ensure that the RCs' educational philosophy is effectively implemented, thus offering an empirical reference for RC education at large.

O' Hara, Robert J. The Collegiate Way: Residential Colleges and the Renewal of Campus Life. https://collegiateway.org/ (last visited May 15, 2021).

Pak Michael S. "The Yale Report of 1828: A New Reading and New Implications. " *History of Education Quarterly*, 2008,48 (1): 30-57.

Penven James, Stephens Robert, Shushok Frank Jr., et al. "The Past, Present, and Future of Residential Colleges." *The Journal of College and University Student Housing*, 2013,39 (2): 114-126.

Pfnister Allan O. "The Role of the Liberal Arts College: A Historical Overview of the Debates." *Journal of Higher Education*, 1984,55 (2): 145-170.

Rudolph Frederick. *The American College and University: A History*. 2nd ed. Athens: University of Georgia Press, 1991.

Rüegg Walter. *A History of the University in Europe:Volume 3, Universities in the Nineteenth and Early Twentieth Centuries (1800—1945)*. Cambridge: Cambridge University Press, 2013.

Thien John R. *A History of American Higher Education*. 3rd ed. Baltimore: Johns Hopkins University Press, 2019.

Walton Linda. *Academies and Society in Southern Sung China*. Honolulu: University of Hawaii Press, 1999.

Watt George. *Living and Learning: Snapshots of Residential College Life at the University of Macau, 2010—2017*. Macau: University of Macau, 2017.

Jaeger Werner. *Paideia: The Ideals of Greek Culture:Volume III* . 2nd ed. Oxford: Oxford University Press, 1986.

Yeoman Henry. *Abbott Lawrence Lowell: 1856—1943*. Cambridge: Harvard University Press, 1948.

参考文献 / Reference

王懿：《中国高等教育改革视域下复旦大学书院的转型与发展》，《高教论坛》2020 年第 9 期。

朱荣贵：《学规与书院教育——以宋代书院为例》，《中国书院》，长沙：湖南教育出版社，1997 年。

李材栋：《白鹿洞书院史略》，北京：教育科学出版社，1989 年。

李伟权、吕静慧、邓宇明：《大一新生对住宿式书院归属感之探索性研究——以澳门大学 C 书院为例》，程海东、宫辉主编：《现
代高校书院制教育研究》，西安：西安交通大学出版社，2016 年。

李国钧主编：《中国书院史》，长沙：湖南教育出版社，1994 年。

孙伟贤、李慧中：《试论住宿书院对学生发展的长远影响：基于对澳门大学蔡继有书院毕业生的访谈研究》，《第六届海峡两岸暨
港澳地区高校现代书院制教育论坛》，上海：复旦大学，2019 年。

高明士：《中国教育制度史论》，台北：台北联经出版事业公司，1999 年。

梁伟贤、刘京京：《探索住宿式书院教育成果的定量评估方法：以澳门大学绍邦书院为例》，《现代高校书院制教育研究 2018 第
五届海峡两岸暨港澳地区高校现代书院制教育论坛优秀论文集》，香港：香港中文大学，2018 年。

陈嘉谷、邓洪波主编：《中国书院史资料》第 3 卷，杭州：浙江教育出版社，1998 年。

陈盘：《春秋的教育》，《"中央研究院"历史语言研究所集刊》第 45 本，1975 年。

程海东：《澳门大学住宿式书院系统成立两年绩效评估（二〇一四年八月至二〇一六年五月）》，程海东、宫辉主编：《现代高校
书院制教育研究》，西安：西安交通大学出版社，2016 年。

黄坤琦：《高校书院育人机制的研究综述与展望》，程海东、宫辉主编：《现代高校书院制教育研究》，西安：西安交通大学出版
社，2016 年。

刘海燕、晏维龙：《回归教育场域：美国大学住宿书院的历史嬗变及启示》，《第六届海峡两岸暨港澳地区高校现代书院制教育论
坛》，上海：复旦大学，2019 年。

刘阳、宋永华、伍宸：《再论书院制：英、美及我国香港顶尖大学书院制模式比较与启示》，《高等教育研究》2018 年第 8 期。

刘虹、张端鸿：《中美综合性大学住宿学院制度比较研究——以耶鲁大学和复旦大学为例》，《河北科技大学学报（社会科学版）》，
2015 年第 3 期。

邓洪波：《中国书院史》，武汉：武汉大学出版社，2012 年。

邓洪波：《岳麓书院志（前言）》，吴道明等修，邓洪波等点校，长沙：岳麓书社，2011 年。

Bowen James. *A History of Western Education:Volume II*. London: Methuen, 1975.

Cohen Arthur M, Kister Carrie B. *The Shaping of American Higher Education: Emergence and Growth of the Contemporary
System*. 2nd ed. Hoboken: John Wiley & Sons, 2009.

Corbeill Anthony. "Education in the Roman Republic: Creating Traditions. " in Yun Lee Too, *Education in Greek and Roman
Antiquity*. Leiden: Brill , 2001.

de Bary Wm Theodore, Chaffee John W. *Neo-Confucian Education: The Formative Stage*. Berkeley: University of California
Press, 1989.

Symoens Hildegarde. *A History of the University in Europe: Volume1, Universities in the Middle Ages*. Cambridge:
Cambridge University Press, 2013.

Duke Alex. *Importing Oxbridge: English Residential Colleges and American Universities*. New Haven: Yale University Press,
1996.

Elman Benjamin. *Education and Society in Late Imperial China, 1600—1900.* Berkeley: University of California Press, 1994.

Griffith Mark. "Public and Private in Early Greek Institutions of Education. " in Yun Lee Too, *Education in Greek and Roman
Antiquity*. Leiden: Brill, 2001.

Haskins Homer Charles. *The Rise of Universities*. Ithaca: Cornell University Press, 1957.

Herbst, Jurgen. "The Yale Report of 1828. " *International Journal of the Classical Tradition*, 2014,11(2): 213-231.

Hutner Gordon, Mohamed Feisal G. *A New Deal for the Humanities: Liberal Arts and the Future of Public Higher Education*.
New Brunswick: Rutgers University Press, 2015.

Lee Thomas H C. *Education in Traditional China: A History*. Leiden: Brill, 2000.

Leff Gordon. *Paris and Oxford Universities in the Thirteenth and Fourteenth Centuries*. New York: Wiley & Sons, 1968.

Lowe Roy. *The History of Higher Education: Major Themes in Education: Volume1,The Origin and Dissemination of the
University Ideal*. London: Routledge, 2009.

Marrou Henri I. *The History of Education in Antiquity*. New York: Heed & Ward, 1956.

Morison Samuel Eliot. *Three Centuries of Harvard*. Cambridge: Harvard University Press, 1936.

01 满珍纪念书院
Moon Chun Memorial College

02 蔡继有书院
Choi Kai Yau College

03 何鸿燊东亚书院
Stanley Ho East Asia College

04 霍英东珍禧书院
Henry Fok Pearl Jubilee College

05 曹光彪书院
Chao Kuang Piu College

06 吕志和书院
Lui Che Woo College

07 郑裕彤书院
Cheng Yu Tung College

08 马万祺罗柏心书院
Ma Man Kei and Lo Pak Sam College

09 张昆仑书院
Cheong Kun Lun College

10 绍邦书院
Shiu Pong College

附　录 / Appendix

近年来，实施书院制已成为高校深化教育改革的重要探索。2014 年，"首届高校现代书院制教育论坛"在北京航空航天大学举行，并成立了高校书院联盟，在加强高校书院交流合作等方面发挥了至关重要的作用，至 2021 年先后举办论坛七次。澳门大学住宿式书院的教学人员在过去八年积极对住宿式书院进行研究，以下是其在书院教育领域的论文和研究成果。

In recent years, the implementation of the residential college system has become an important area of research in higher education sector. In 2014, the "First Educational Forum on Modern Residential College System" was held at Beihang University and the League of Residential College Education was established playing a crucial role in strengthening exchanges and cooperation between higher education institutes. By 2021, seven forums had been organised. Academic staff of University of Macau Residential College have been actively involved in residential college researches in the past eight years. The followings are the papers and research outcomes of the residential college academic team in the field of residential college education.

何敬恩、齐亚宁、李艳琪，等：《潜在课程与自我成长及人际关系研究：以澳门大学蔡继有书院个案为例》，官辉、苏玉波、叶明编：《现代高校书院制教育研究 2017：第四届海峡两岸暨港澳地区高校现代书院制教育论坛优秀论文集》，西安：西安交通大学出版社，2017 年。

李可、吴怡、苑爽：《文化交流活动对书院生领导力影响之研究：以曹光彪书院暑期文化交流项目为例》，《现代高校书院制教育研究 2018：第五届海峡两岸暨港澳地区高校现代书院制教育论坛优秀论文集》，香港：香港中文大学，2018 年。

李可：《朋辈教育与书院创业教育模式构建》，《第六届海峡两岸暨港澳地区高校现代书院制教育论坛》，上海：复旦大学，2019 年。

李可：《澳门大学书院的多元文化教育责任与挑战》，官辉、苏玉波、叶明编：《现代高校书院制教育研究 2017：第四届海峡两岸暨港澳地区高校现代书院制教育论坛优秀论文集》，西安：西安交通大学出版社，2017 年。

李伟权、吕静慧、邓宇明：《大一新生对住宿式书院归属感之探索性研究：以澳门大学 C 书院为例》，程海东、宫辉主编：《现代高校书院制教育研究》，西安：西安交通大学出版社，2016 年。

林仲桂、齐亚宁：《澳门大学蔡继有书院学生社团新型管理模式：书院导师宏观指导与学生自主管理》，《现代高校书院制教育研究 2018：第五届海峡两岸暨港澳地区高校现代书院制教育论坛优秀论文集》，香港：香港中文大学，2018 年。

林仲桂、颜轲越、齐亚宁：〈澳门大学蔡继有书院基于大数据分析的院生管理新模式〉，《第六届海峡两岸暨港澳地区高校现代书院制教育论坛》，上海：复旦大学，2019 年。

孙伟贤、李慧中：《试论住宿书院对学生发展的长远影响：基于对澳门大学蔡继有书院毕业生的访谈研究》，《第六届海峡两岸暨港澳地区高校现代书院制教育论坛》，上海：复旦大学，2019 年。

张俏婷、李慧中：《"大鱼"与"小鱼"的互动交往：从澳门大学蔡继有书院的师生关系说起》，《第六届海峡两岸暨港澳地区高校现代书院制教育论坛》，上海：复旦大学，2019 年。

张美芳、黄才试、孙斯斯：《在书院生活中培养学生的中华文化价值观：以澳门大学张昆仑书院为例》，《第六届海峡两岸暨港澳地区高校现代书院制教育论坛》，上海：复旦大学，2019 年。

梁青宁、许德宝：《书院模式下推行礼貌诚信教育的尝试和初步成效：以澳门大学马万祺罗柏心书院为例》，《第六届海峡两岸暨港澳地区高校现代书院制教育论坛》，上海：复旦大学，2019 年。

梁伟贤、刘京京：《在住宿式书院的体验式学习中贯彻全人教育》，官辉、苏玉波、叶明编：《现代高校书院制教育研究 2017：第四届海峡两岸暨港澳地区高校现代书院制教育论坛优秀论文集》，西安：西安交通大学出版社，2017 年。

梁伟贤、刘京京：《探索住宿式书院教育成果的定量评估方法：以澳门大学绍邦书院为例》，《现代高校书院制教育研究 2018 第五届海峡两岸暨港澳地区高校现代书院制教育论坛优秀论文集》，香港：香港中文大学，2018 年。

许恒嘉、黄兆琳、梁青宁，等：《以澳门大学书院实践经验为本论书院导师专业特性与其发展》，《现代高校书院制教育研究 2018 第五届海峡两岸暨港澳地区高校现代书院制教育论坛优秀论文集》，香港：香港中文大学，2018 年。

许恒嘉：《书院生心智发展与实践行动的映射：澳门大学曹光彪书院驻院导师对书院教育设计的认识》，程海东、宫辉主编：《现代高校书院制教育研究》，西安：西安交通大学出版社，2016 年。

许恒嘉：《书院导师以织锦式辅导架构陪伴院生共构心智发展的轨迹》，官辉、苏玉波、叶明编：《现代高校书院制教育研究 2017：第四届海峡两岸暨港澳地区高校现代书院制教育论坛优秀论文集》，西安：西安交通大学出版社，2017 年。

程海东：《建设现代高校书院的重要元素》，官辉、苏玉波、叶明编：《现代高校书院制教育研究 2016：第四届海峡两岸暨港澳地区高校现代书院制教育论坛优秀论文集》，西安：西安交通大学出版社，2016 年。

程海东：《澳门大学住宿式书院系统成立两年绩效评估（二○一四年八月至二○一六年五月）》，程海东、宫辉主编：《现代高校书院制教育研究》，西安：西安交通大学出版社，2016 年。

黄兆琳、蒋怡、陈伟江：《从 Facebook、微信到 APP：澳门大学霍英东珍禧书院师生在线互动关系的发展》，宫辉、苏玉波、叶明编：

《现代高校书院制教育研究 2017：第四届海峡两岸暨港澳地区高校现代书院制教育论坛优秀论文集》，西安：西安交通大学出版社，2017 年。

黄兆琳、蒋怡：《住宿式书院"统合式"服务学习教育模式研究》，张军、武立勋、董卓宁、邵明英编：《现代高校书院制教育研究》，北京：北京航空航天大学出版社，2015 年。

黄兆琳、蒋怡：《住宿式书院"统合式"教育模式的发展：以澳门大学霍英东珍禧书院 2015—2016 年度才智精进项目为例》，程海东、宫辉主编：《现代高校书院制教育研究》，西安：西安交通大学出版社，2016 年。

温慧珊、黄才试：《生活、服务、学习：四川地震灾后山区服务学习项目成效》，张军、武立勋、董卓宁、邵明英编：《现代高校书院制教育研究》，北京：北京航空航天大学出版社，2015 年。

褚彩霞、冯浩贤、李洪德：《书院心理辅导模式探索：书院导师的心理辅导角色》，官辉、苏玉波、叶明编：《现代高校书院制教育研究 2017：第四届海峡两岸暨港澳地区高校现代书院制教育论坛优秀论文集》，西安：西安交通大学出版社，2017 年。

褚彩霞：《书院开展服务学习教育的效果与经验：以澳门大学吕志和书院服务学习项目为例》，程海东、宫辉主编：《现代高校书院制教育研究》，西安：西安交通大学出版社，2016 年。

褚彩霞：《澳门大学吕志和书院肯尼亚服务学习初探》，《第六届海峡两岸暨港澳地区高校现代书院制教育论坛》，上海：复旦大学，2019 年。

齐亚宁、王春明、赵静：《"交互式"师资配置模式下住宿式书院与院系间合作：以澳门大学蔡继有书院为例》，程海东、宫辉主编：《现代高校书院制教育研究》，西安：西安交通大学出版社，2016 年。

刘京京、于梦：《探索构建以"学习、沟通、移情、创新、领袖"五种能力为特色的书院教育体系》，张军、武立勋、董卓宁、邵明英编：《现代高校书院制教育研究》，北京：北京航空航天大学出版社，2015 年。

刘京京、张本梓、陈锦翔：《绍邦书院学生活动质量的影响因素初探：基于 132 个活动的定量分析》，《第六届海峡两岸暨港澳地区高校现代书院制教育论坛》，上海：复旦大学，2019 年。

刘京京、梁伟贤、刘颖聪，等：《探索构建以"长期性、定期性活动"为核心的书院体验式教育》，程海东、宫辉主编：《现代高校书院制教育研究》，西安：西安交通大学出版社，2016 年。

刘振钊：《住宿式书院：通过"小小程序员"推动服务学习数字化以辅助城乡科技教育落差》，《第六届海峡两岸暨港澳地区高校现代书院制教育论坛》，上海：复旦大学，2019 年。

潘晓彤、齐亚宁：《体验式学习在住宿式书院中的具体实行》，张军、武立勋、董卓宁、邵明英编：《现代高校书院制教育研究》，北京：北京航空航天大学出版社，2015 年。

蒋怡：《从行动力到领导力：学生领导才能在服务学习项目中的发展》，《第六届海峡两岸暨港澳地区高校现代书院制教育论坛》，上海：复旦大学，2019 年。

庞百腾：《书院的国际化角色》，官辉、苏玉波、叶明编：《现代高校书院制教育研究 2017：第四届海峡两岸暨港澳地区高校现代书院制教育论坛优秀论文集》，西安：西安交通大学出版社，2017 年。

程海东：《澳门大学住宿式书院系统成立两年绩效评估（二〇一四年八月至二〇一六年五月）》，程海东、官辉、钟玲、张爱萍编：《现代高校书院制教育研究》，西安：西安交通大学出版社，2016 年。

程海东：《建设现代高校书院的重要元素》，官辉、苏玉波、叶明编：《现代高校书院制教育研究 2016：第四届海峡两岸暨港澳地区高校现代书院制教育论坛优秀论文集》，西安：西安交通大学出版社，2016 年。

褚彩霞、冯浩贤、李洪德：《书院心理辅导模式探索：书院导师的心理辅导角色》，官辉、苏玉波、叶明编：《现代高校书院制教育研究 2017：第四届海峡两岸暨港澳地区高校现代书院制教育论坛优秀论文集》，西安：西安交通大学出版社，2017 年。

褚彩霞：《澳门大学吕志和书院肯尼亚服务学习初探》，《第六届海峡两岸暨港澳地区高校现代书院制教育论坛》，上海：复旦大学，2019 年。

褚彩霞：《澳门大学书院教育发展与反思——以吕志和书院为例》，甘阳、孙向晨主编：《通识教育评论》，上海：复旦大学，2017 年。

褚彩霞：《书院教育中的多元群体融合》，《第七届高校现代书院制教育论坛论文集》，威海：哈尔滨工业大学，2021 年。

褚彩霞：《书院开展服务学习教育的效果与经验：以澳门大学吕志和书院服务学习项目为例》，程海东、官辉、钟玲、张爱萍编：《现代高校书院制教育研究》，西安：西安交通大学出版社，2016 年。

何敬恩、齐亚宁、李艳琪，等：《潜在课程与自我成长及人际关系研究：以澳门大学蔡继有书院个案为例》，官辉、苏玉波、叶明编：《现代高校书院制教育研究 2017：第四届海峡两岸暨港澳地区高校现代书院制教育论坛优秀论集》，西安：西安交通大学出版社，2017 年。

黄兆琳、蒋怡、陈伟江：《从 Facebook、微信到 APP：澳门大学霍英东珍禧书院师生在线互动关系的发展》，官辉、苏玉波、叶明编：《现代高校书院制教育研究 2017：第四届海峡两岸暨港澳地区高校现代书院制教育论坛优秀论文集》，西安：西安交通大学出版社，2017 年。

黄兆琳、蒋怡：《住宿式书院"统合式"服务学习教育模式研究》，张军、武立勋、董卓宁，等编：《现代高校书院制教育研究》，北京：北京航空航天大学出版社，2015 年。

黄兆琳、蒋怡：《住宿式书院"统合式"教育模式的发展：以澳门大学霍英东珍禧书院 2015~2016 年度才智精进项目为例》，程海东、官辉、钟玲，等编：《现代高校书院制教育研究》，西安：西安交通大学出版社，2016 年。

蒋怡：《从行动力到领导力：学生领导才能在服务学习项目中的发展》，《第六届海峡两岸暨港澳地区高校现代书院制教育论坛》，上海：复旦大学，2019 年。

蒋怡：《书院课外活动，学术成长的助力还是阻力？——对住宿式书院课外活动与学术成绩的关系研究》，《新时代 新发展——第七届高校现代书院制教育论坛》，威海：哈尔滨工业大学，2021 年。

李可、吴怡、苑爽：《文化交流活动对书院生领导力影响之研究：以曹光彪书院暑期文化交流项目为例》，《现代高校书院制教育研究 2018 第五届海峡两岸暨港澳地区高校现代书院制教育论坛优秀论文集》，香港：香港中文大学，2018 年。

李可：《澳门大学书院的多元文化教育责任与挑战》，官辉、苏玉波、叶明编：《现代高校书院制教育研究 2017：第四届海峡两岸暨港澳地区高校现代书院制教育论坛优秀论文集》，西安：西安交通大学出版社，2017 年。

李可：《朋辈教育与书院创业教育模式构建》，《第六届海峡两岸暨港澳地区高校现代书院制教育论坛》，上海：复旦大学，2019 年。

李伟权、吕静慧、邓宇明：《大一新生对住宿式书院归属感之探索性研究：以澳门大学 C 书院为例》，程海东、官辉、钟玲，等编：《现代高校书院制教育研究》，西安：西安交通大学出版社，2016 年。

梁青宁、许德宝：《书院模式下推行礼貌诚信教育的尝试和初步成效：以澳门大学马万祺罗柏心书院为例》，《第六届海峡两岸暨港澳地区高校现代书院制教育论坛》，上海：复旦大学，2019 年。

梁伟贤、刘京京：《探索住宿式书院教育成果的定量评估方法：以澳门大学绍邦书院为例》，《现代高校书院制教育研究 2018 第五届海峡两岸暨港澳地区高校现代书院制教育论坛优秀论文集》，香港：香港中文大学，2018 年。

梁伟贤、刘京京：《在住宿式书院的体验式学习中贯彻全人教育》，官辉、苏玉波、叶明编：《现代高校书院制教育研究 2017：第四届海峡两岸暨港澳地区高校现代书院制教育论坛优秀论文集》，西安：西安交通大学出版社，2017 年。

林仲桂、齐亚宁：《澳门大学蔡继有书院学生社团新型管理模式：书院导师宏观指导与学生自主管理》，《现代高校书院制教育研究 2018 第五届海峡两岸暨港澳地区高校现代书院制教育论坛优秀论文集》，香港：香港中文大学，2018 年。

林仲桂、颜轲越、齐亚宁：《澳门大学蔡继有书院基于大数据分析的院生管理新模式》，《第六届海峡两岸暨港澳地区高校现代书院制教育论坛》，上海：复旦大学，2019 年。

刘京京、张本梓、陈锦翎，等：《住宿式书院学生人际网络的定量分析初探——基于社会网络分析》，《第七届高校现代书院制教育论坛论文集》，威海：哈尔滨大学（威海）出版社，2021 年。

刘京京、梁伟贤、刘颖聪，等：《探索构建以"长期性、定期性活动"为核心的书院体验式教育》，程海东、官辉、钟玲，等编：《现代高校书院制教育研究》，西安：西安交通大学出版社，2016 年。

刘京京、于梦：《探索构建以"学习、沟通、移情、创新、领袖"五种能力为特色的书院教育体系》，张军、武立勋、董卓宁，等编：《现代高校书院制教育研究》，北京：北京航空航天大学出版社，2015 年。

刘京京、张本梓、陈锦翎：《绍邦书院学生活动质量的影响因素初探：基于 132 个活动的定量分析》，《第六届海峡两岸暨港澳地区高校现代书院制教育论坛》，上海：复旦大学，2019 年。

刘沛棋：《文化育人："文化育航"》，《第七届高校现代书院制教育论坛优秀论文集》，威海：哈尔滨大学（威海）出版社，2021 年。

刘振钊：《住宿式书院：通过 "小小程序员"推动服务学习数字化以辅助城乡科技教育落差》，《第六届海峡两岸暨港澳地区高校现代书院制教育论坛》，上海：复旦大学，2019 年。

潘晓彤、齐亚宁：《体验式学习在住宿式书院中的具体实行》，张军、武立勋、董卓宁，等编：《现代高校书院制教育研究》，北京：北京航空航天大学出版社，2015 年。

庞百腾：《书院的国际化角色》，官辉、苏玉波、叶明编：《现代高校书院制教育研究 2017：第四届海峡两岸暨港澳地区高校现代书院制教育论坛优秀论文集》，西安：西安交通大学出版社，2017 年。

齐亚宁、王春明、赵静：《"交互式"师资配置模式下住宿式书院与院系间合作：以澳门大学蔡继有书院为例》，程海东、官辉、钟玲，等编：《现代高校书院制教育研究》，西安：西安交通大学出版社，2016 年。

孙伟贤、李慧中：《试论住宿书院对学生发展的长远影响：基于对澳门大学蔡继有书院毕业生的访谈研究》，《第六届海峡两岸暨港澳地区高校现代书院制教育论坛》，上海：复旦大学，2019 年。

温慧珊、黄才试：《生活、服务、学习：四川地震灾后山区服务学习项目成效》，张军、武立勋、董卓宁，等编：《现代高校书院制教育研究》，北京：北京航空航天大学出版社，2015 年。

许恒嘉、黄兆琳、梁青宁，等：《以澳门大学书院实践经验为本论书院导师专业特性与其发展》，《现代高校书院制教育研究 2018 第五届海峡两岸暨港澳地区高校现代书院制教育论坛优秀论文集》，香港：香港中文大学，2018 年。

许恒嘉：《书院导师以织锦式辅导架构陪伴院生共构心智发展的轨迹》，官辉、苏玉波、叶明编：《现代高校书院制教育研究 2017：第四届海峡两岸暨港澳地区高校现代书院制教育论坛优秀论文集》，西安：西安交通大学出版社，2017 年。

许恒嘉：《书院生心智发展与实践行动的映射：澳门大学曹光彪书院驻院导师对书院教育设计的认识》，程海东、官辉、钟玲，等编：《现代高校书院制教育研究》，西安：西安交通大学出版社，2016 年。

张美芳、褚彩霞、林雪仪，等：《把住宿式书院打造成社群教育平台——以澳门大学张昆仑书院为例》，《第七届高校现代书院制教育论坛论文集》，威海：哈尔滨大学（威海）出版社，2021 年。

张美芳、黄才试、孙斯斯：《在书院生活中培养学生的中华文化价值观：以澳门大学张昆仑书院为例》，《第六届海峡两岸暨港澳地区高校现代书院制教育论坛》，上海：复旦大学，2019 年。

张俏婷、李慧中：《"大鱼"与"小鱼"的互动交往：从澳门大学蔡继有书院的师生关系说起》，《第六届海峡两岸暨港澳地区高校现代书院制教育论坛》，上海：复旦大学，2019 年。

郑智明、吴崇旗：《户外冒险教育课程对澳门大学生生活效能与团队凝聚力之成效》：《公民教育与活动领导学报第二十六辑》，台北：台湾师范大学，2021 年。

Evans Martyn, Kevin Thompson. "Visits to Four Collegiate Universities." *A Collegiate Way: A Voice for Collegiate Universities Around the World*, 2016(2): 1-14.

Thompson Kevin. "Checking Out of Hôtel California: Blinking in Post-Pandemic First Light." *Collegiate Way International,* 2020(1): 5-8.

Evans Martyn, Burt T P. *The Collegiate Way: University Education in a Collegiate Context*. Rotterdam, Netherlands: Sense Publishers, 2016.

Evans, Thompson. "Visits to Four Collegiate Universities." A Collegiate Way: A Voice for Collegiate Universities Around the World, vol.2 (2016), pp. 1-14.

Lee, Tang and Lu. "Service Learning Project of CYTC in Melaka Portuguese Settlement, Malaysia." Journal of Service Learning and Social Engagement, vol.1(2018), pp. 81- 86.

Lu, Chen and Yang. "Introductory Service-Learning Experience: Macau College Students in Ethnic Minority School of Mountain Area in China." Metropolitan Universities Journal, vol.3(2019), pp. 10-19.

Thompson. "Checking Out of Hôtel California: Blinking in Post-Pandemic First Light." Collegiate Way International, vol.1 (2020), pp. 5-8.

Thompson. In The Collegiate Way: University Education in a Collegiate Context, ed. Evans, Burt, Rotterdam, Netherlands: Sense Publishers, 2016, pp.7-11.

Thompson. In The Collegiate Way: University Education in a Collegiate Context, ed. Evans, Burt, Rotterdam, Netherlands: Sense Publishers, 2016, pp.57-60.

Wan. "Enhancing University of Macau students' community engagement through residential college programs in partnership with local non-governmental organizations." Merrill, Chang and Islam, Education and Sustainability: Paradigms, Policies and Practices in Asia, Singapore: Routledge, 2017, pp. 258-269.

Wong. "Service learning with live broadcasting technology: An online voluntary teaching project in University of Macau Henry Fok Pearl Jubilee College." The Hong Kong Polytechnic University eLearning Forum Asia eLFA2017 Conference Proceedings, 2017.

Yeung, Wan. "How to engage students in online teaching material? The making of an e-learning programme for university resident assistants." EDULEARN20 Proceedings, 2020.

Yu, Sun. "Promising Practice: International Communication and Learning Program." Tamara, Brett, Internationalizing US Student Affairs Practice: An Intercultural and Inclusive Framework , New York: Routledge, 2018, p. 66.